GROOMING
— *the* NEXT —
GENERATION
— *for* —
SUCCESS™

BOOKS BY DANI JOHNSON

Spirit Driven Success

AVAILABLE FROM DESTINY IMAGE PUBLISHERS

GROOMING
— *the* NEXT —
GENERATION
— *for* —
SUCCESS™

DANI JOHNSON

Previously Published by Call To Freedom Int'l, LLC Nevada Limited Liability Company; copyright 2008; ISBN: 978-0-9789551-4-4

DESTINY IMAGE® PUBLISHERS, INC.

P.O. Box 310, Shippensburg, PA 17257-0310

"Speaking to the Purposes of God for This Generation and for the Generations to Come."

This book and all other Destiny Image, Revival Press, MercyPlace, Fresh Bread, Destiny Image Fiction, and Treasure House books are available at Christian bookstores and distributors worldwide.

For a U.S. bookstore nearest you, call 1-800-722-6774.

For more information on foreign distributors, call 717-532-3040.

Reach us on the Internet: www.destinyimage.com.

ISBN 10: 0-7684-3155-7
ISBN 13: 978-0-7684-3155-1

For Worldwide Distribution, Printed in the U.S.A.

3 4 5 6 7 8 9 10 11 / 13 12 11

DEDICATION

To every human being who has a desire to see this next generation succeed in all areas of their lives. Thank you for being willing to do your part.

ACKNOWLEDGMENTS

Thank you to the Creator of the heavens and the earth, my Father in Heaven who whispered, nudged, pushed, stirred, and made it so obvious to me that I should do this project. Thank You for Your Word. Thank You for always fulfilling Your Word. Thank You for teaching me all You have taught me. Apart from You, I am nothing and can do nothing.

Hans, my amazing husband. You have always spurred me on beyond what I thought I could do. Thank you for creating the platform for the many messages that are in this mouth to be heard. Thank you for being so patient with me all these years.

Kristina, Arika, Cabe, Roman, and Micah: You are all so amazing. What a blessing you have been in our lives; I've learned so much from each of you. I couldn't ask for a better "tribe." Thank you for loving me and being so good, obedient, and teachable. You have set examples for many to follow.

Aunt Marie: Thank you so much for how you have encouraged me through the years and how you have pointed out what I was doing that was working. I love you very much, and I am so grateful for you.

The DJC Team: You are amazing to us. Thank you for your dedication, excellence, and patience. Thank you for believing in the vision of impacting people's lives and for doing it, as well.

Donna Taylor: You are wonderful to work with— talented, organized, and awesome at reaching deadlines with a spirit of excellence.

This project obviously would not be done without you. You really are a gift from God.

Jack and Lavonne: Thank you for always encouraging me and speaking truth and wisdom into my life.

DJC Clients who have such a hunger to grow and not to settle for less: I am so blessed for how you have grabbed all the information we have given you, and I'm thrilled that you are becoming examples to all those around you.

Beth Johnson, thank for your awesome example and for all the years of inspiration. I am so grateful for your words of encouragement as well as your allowing me to be a part of your kids' life. You trusted me to influence them, and it showed me a deep maturity we should all have in knowing that others will influence our kids. Your trust in God is profound to me.

Grandpa and Grandma Johnson, you were the first loving family I had ever encountered; it changed me to my core. You gave me a goal for what I wanted for the generations that we were birthing. I thank you for your marriage, the talks of persistence, and the value of family. Without your example I certainly wouldn't be married or even care about the next generation.

Grandpa and Grandma Jackson, thank you for your persistent prayers for your children's children. I am truly blessed as a result. Your marriage of over 50 years has set an example for all of us to follow. Thank you for that heritage.

TESTIMONIALS

Dani's tips were so practical! ...Dani clarified things for me in such a way that I get it now! For the first time, I feel that we have a clear direction with our parenting. This has been a lifesaver for me, my kids, *and* our family and future as a whole! *Thank you so much, Dani.*

—CARLA DOLLAR

I am a 50-year-old grandmother of nine who was totally blown away by the information I heard. You totally captured my attention by your passion, the depth, and most of all, the quality of information that you shared. Thank you, Dani, for providing the answers to questions that I've had all these years. Your *Grooming the Next Generation for Success* is phenomenal! Everyone needs to hear it over and over.

—PAMELA KUNZE

I love this program. It really inspired me to get back on track with my kids. There were a lot of things that I was letting slide, and I didn't realize how much I was hindering their future success as adults. Thank you so much for your wonderful insight. It has helped my family already.

—KIM LOPICCOLO

You hit the nail on the head. Adding this content to our library is priceless.

—SANDRA CAREY

I love that your principles transfer throughout business, parenting, and marriage.

—LORI PANKRATZ

The program was great. We already have taken many steps to limit the exposure that our daughter receives, but we were not aware how big of a problem pornography is in the U.S. among younger people. The best advice we got was how to discipline kids with the mindset of protection and not control.

—DANNI HANKINS

I actually used the word "honor" tonight and the kids apologized after they thought about their words to each other. Thank you, Dani.

—LISA

Dani, *wow! Thank you* for your vision, passion, and strength.

—CAROLE BLOMGREN

I'm a home-school mom and I have great kids. But *wow,* I learned so much, things I hadn't even thought about, like teaching my children to honor each other so they will know how to honor their spouses.

—MICHELLE DAYE

One eye-opening aspect of the training was how the same Expose, Involve, and Advance process that works in business also works with raising kids. You made it plain to see why it is *so* important to safeguard our kids by making sure they are exposed to the right messages, not what's so prevalent in the world. Dani, thanks again.

—BOB SKIFFINGTON

Dani is so amazing. I started to apply some of the things Dani taught. Dani's right! Our kids want to do good. She has helped me see what I have done well and the areas I need to work on. I love her passion and willingness to tell us like it is. Thank you for impacting *every* part of my life.

—Kathy Humphreys

This program was affirming and challenging all at the same time.

—Anonymous

Dani, my husband and I were absolutely riveted, convicted, inspired, and empowered…all at the same time. Today we started applying what we learned, and *wow!* We had amazing results right away with our two kids. We just were struggling with some arguing starting with our 7-year-old, and disobeying and screaming with our 3-year-old. We were always trying to be proactive parents, but really felt we lacked a lot of skills and tools to effectively handle things. Now we feel empowered and effective with tools that won't encourage rebellion. God bless you, Dani!

—Larissa Wheeler

I am a single mom of three and I learned so much. I am encouraged and filled with hope. With this information, I can do a better job with my 8-year-old daughter. Thank you from the bottom of my heart.

—Rebecca Fischer

CONTENTS

We all have natural abilities, gifts, and talents. Dani Johnson's gift is her ability to clearly explain the skills needed for building success and wealth. She has discovered that the same principles she teaches in her business seminars that have made clients successful are the same principles for grooming the next generation for success. As a multi-millionaire and entrepreneur of five companies, she imparts her personal wisdom, knowledge, and experience in *Grooming the Next Generation for Success.*

I love Dani's heart and passion for wanting to pass on the skills she has honed over the years of her success—skills such as financial responsibility, growing finances, building strong relationships, understanding people, and so much more. My mom and dad were not business people, so I can't blame them for the challenges I've had in my life. But I can tell you with great confidence that if I had been trained up in the knowledge now available through this book, there is no question that much of my time, energy, and money would have been saved.

That's why this book is so important. It goes beyond the best we all know how to do and equips us and the next generation to succeed in every area of our lives. I know my two daughters will make better choices because they understand the secrets Dani reveals to make them responsible and able to take advantage of every opportunity that comes with financial and personal success.

Grooming the Next Generation for Success reaches the next generation now and trains them on the fundamentals of success that are critical to the financial choices they will make in the future that could impact them for years. Knowing the fundamentals, by the time a child reaches adulthood, success becomes something understood and woven into their very being and fiber so that instead of fumbling their way through life, success becomes a natural experience rather than a fortunate accident.

STEPHEN BALDWIN

Through the years we have been stopped at restaurants, on airplanes, in grocery stores, and in just about every public place you can think of, by people commending us on the conduct of our kids. Often someone asks, "Do you teach parenting classes?" or "Have you written a book on parenting?"

My answer has always been no, but that changed last year when we published *Grooming the Next Generation for Success* Home Study Course, after our clients and other well-intentioned people provoked us in this direction—and that's why this book is in your hands right now.

For instance, a few years ago at a doctor's office, I received another compliment. I was there with our then 14-year-old daughter and three young sons aged 11, 8, and 6. Our daughter hurt her arm during a soccer game and getting her quickly to a medical facility was my primary concern. Because it was high season for injuries and illnesses, the place was packed full.

After taking one look at us, the nurse said, "You can't bring all those kids in the examination room."

"Well then, I'll have to take my business elsewhere, ma'am," I answered, "because I'm sorry, but I will not leave these three boys here alone."

"I'm not sure if the doctor's going to OK this," she answered with a mean attitude. "But go ahead to the back."

We sat down in a tiny little box of an examination room—four children, one chair, and one examination table.

The nurse came in, took a look, and was flabbergasted. The doctor comes in, already on guard because the previous room had a couple of boys the same age as two of ours, who were anything but nice. We could hear them through the walls. They were wild, disrespectful, mean-spirited, and dishonorable to the doctor and their parents because they were allowed to misbehave.

"No! I don't want to! No! Don't touch me! No! I don't like you!"

So she walks into our room with preconceived notions and her dukes up. *This is going to be hell!* she thought. To her amazement, our sons didn't say a word; they just sat quietly doing their homework throughout Arika's examination. When it was over, the doctor said, "I have to be honest with you, Mrs. Johnson. I am absolutely impressed. In all my years in this profession, I've never come across children such as yours."

We walked into the lobby, and the other doctor and nurses expressed the same sentiments. "Wow! We expected the worst out of this situation, but your children are so well-behaved."

They were giving our sons high-fives, and then began saying the same things I've heard over and over, "Do you teach classes?"

"Oh, man! We've been through hell with some of these children."

"You've got to teach people in this community how to raise their children—yours have been just great."

All I could say is, "Thank you so much for your encouragement… I'm humbled by your comments."

After we were all in the car, I thanked our kids for setting such good examples and for giving the staffers in the medical facility a different opinion about kids in general. Driving home I was reminded of the many times that others had made comments or asked me for help. In fact, Diana is probably the most memorable. She is the mother of one of my son's friends. Our conversation went something like this...

"Who is this?" I asked.

"This is Diana."

Diana...who? I thought.

"Andrew's mother."

"Oh!" (I didn't know who Andrew was right off the bat, so I was trying to connect the dots.)

"We were at Cabe's birthday party last year."

"OK." (I thought, *Yearbook. Oh, OK. Andrew.*)

"I say to my son everyday, 'Why can't you be more like Cabe?'"

I thought, *What a terrible thing to say to your second-grade son.*

"Your children honor you. Every time my son talks back to me, I say, 'Cabe wouldn't do that to his mother, so why are you doing that to me?'"

I soon discovered that this woman had four out-of-control children (three young boys and a mouthy, pre-adolescent daughter).

"Let's meet at my home, and we'll work on it together."

She agreed.

We've all made mistakes, but this parent was crying out for help. After a little while and a few tips, she (and her children) now have awesome relationships.

—————✎—————

The tips and techniques we used to make raising kids less stressful and more successful, are now in your hands.

We are not claiming to be experts with all the answers. We aren't saying that we're perfect parents and your results are going to be perfect. But we do have five kids, and we want to share with you the specific "how-to's" based on real-life scenarios that really worked for us and our clients.

This information will increase your children's odds of succeeding in their future careers, as spouses, as parents, and as responsible community people. I believe we all want the best for our kids and yet many times are unsure how to ensure that the best will happen for them. I know that this book can effectively change lives and restore relationships.

So if you have your hands or fingerprints on the *next generation* in some way, shape, or form, this book is intended for you. Depending on your personal and professional involvement, it's possible that you can positively impact one, three, five, twenty, or thousands of children and change the course of their lives forever. We've received thousands of testimonials from clients who've put these teachings into practice and have received great results. Some of the testimonials prompted by attending our live seminars you'll read later in this book, but two in particular, I'd like to share right now.

"We have two boys, 15 and 12," write Kurt and Julie. "We think we're pretty good parents, but we had our eyes opened up a bit more this evening. We have always intended to raise our children to be their very best, and now we have a few more tools in the tool box. We *loved* the way you described the difference between protection and control…*wow!* It makes perfect sense."

Michele writes, "As a mother of seven children (15, 13, 10, 9, 5, 2, and 1), I needed to hear this fifteen years ago. I read parenting books, listened to parenting CDs, and have attended parenting classes. Nothing has made more sense than the information you shared. I want my kids to grow up to be successful, honorable, and respectful to others and to care more about giving than getting. You shared how simply it can be done. *Thank you!* Your information has blessed my family's life forever. Thanks for providing us with the information we need to be the best parents, spouses, and business builders we can be."

This is the impact I'm talking about. As parents, grandparents, educators, and social workers seize the opportunity to empower their children for success, they'll see lives and futures transformed. There is plenty of information out there—CDs, DVDs, and books on disciplining children, but I haven't come across any materials regarding *grooming them for success*. **The success I'm talking about is a holistic approach incorporating the spiritual, physical, emotional, mental, relational, and financial realms.**

Unfortunately, many haven't experienced success and are still trying to figure it out for themselves. As a result, they don't know how to bring it into their children's lives. That's OK. I've been working on this concept for almost 20 years and have purposely raised our children with this mindset. Also, we have received tens of thousands of written testimonials from our clients who are now earning 6- and 7-figure incomes due to our training.

What I've found in the marketplace, though, is that most successful people aren't really thinking about grooming their *next generation*. This, I believe, has caused our nation as a whole to suffer in a few different areas. Instead of grooming our kids for success, we are grooming them for absolute mediocrity, and a generation of apathetic kids without drive, dreams, or direction is being raised. And if these unfortunate kids have parents who've sacrificed them on the altar of their own personal success, then these children also have entitlement issues, which is an attitude of expecting something for nothing. How sad is that?

GENTLE WARNING

This is a good place for a warning—your feathers may be ruffled while reading this book, so accept my apologies in advance. Some of this content will definitely rub you the wrong way, but allow me to disarm you right now so that you won't be defensive later with my teachings. Our parenting principles may shock you. But they work, and we get results to prove it.

Please be willing to hear. Be willing to explore. Be willing to look at other possibilities.

Here's another disclosure. My husband and I didn't grow up in the best of circumstances, which we will discuss later. Much of what we learned has come from studying the Bible—*the* Answer Book. (The Bible is the best "success" book ever written. Every success book written after it simply takes its principles, changes the font, renames it, and then—boom—calls it their own.

There are profound principles in the Bible. Principles for succeeding in relationships, parenting, government, leadership, war, health, solving difficult problems, as well as overcoming poverty and how to become wealthy. I encourage you to read it cover to cover without the confines of religious opinions attached. You will be amazed at how much wisdom is in this phenomenal Book.

We've also had some good coaching along the way. Since parenting and successfully raising our children has been a topic of interest for me ever since I became a mother, every time I'd see successful kids, I'd naturally ask their successful parents, "What's the secret to your success? What did you do?" Only those techniques that we've learned, applied, and have actually worked for us will be shared in this book.

So open your mind to the *big* picture so it will be easier to do *big* picture things. Be open-minded. I'm a *big* picture thinker and a down-the-road kind of girl, which means I'm future-minded. As business owners, which is how we earn our living, it's mandatory to have a *big* picture vision for every area of our lives. (I've learned this tip from being in business since the age of 19, although I certainly was not "equipped" at that age to be in business. I'll tell you a little bit about that in the following chapters.)

In this book, we're writing from the perspective of business owners who've personally coached tens of thousands of people for years and have seen the hindrances groomed into them when they were children.

These hindrances are causing them to fail and to make poor decisions in all areas of their lives.

Let's not set our kids up for failure, but for success! This is the perspective that we are writing from because I've personally suffered from the poor skills groomed into me that eventually set me up for failure. The failure was not just in business, but in all areas of my life: career, spiritual, relational, and physical.

As adults, as parents, and as influencers over younger people, we should not want to equip our children poorly. The question we should ask ourselves constantly is: how can we give it our best shot to set them up for success and not failure?

COMMON SENSE

Having common sense now and for the future is also important because what I see happening today makes me angry. My anger is not directed at anyone in particular, but in general. We have to do something individually and collectively about this national trend of ignoring the problems our children are facing. If we don't violently take back what's ours and get out there to fight for our kids, there are going to be bigger problems coming down the pipeline than anything we've ever experienced as a society.

When I talk about common sense for the future, I'm talking about parents being proactive to prevent being reactive later. (This includes teachers at school or at church, grandparents, and anyone with influence over this *next generation*.) I'm talking about equipping children for success now. I'm talking about setting them up for success by design, instead of failing by default.

Today, we're seeing a generation of kids with no regard for anyone in authority. How has this come upon us? They are going crazy killing each other, their parents, grandparents, teachers—and this is not right. School systems are messed up. Television is messed up. Music is messed up.

But what can I do? I'm just one person.

You can do a lot. I believe that helping one home at a time can make a huge difference. One family can influence another by pointing them in the right direction. For example, look at Cabe's influence with his classmate. I had no idea that his influence would cause a parent to ask her son, "Why can't you be more like Cabe?" She compared the honor and respect that Cabe had for me with the total lack of respect her son had for her.

When perfect strangers compliment, and extended family members notice the change and comment, this is influence at its best.

It only takes a few good people to step up and start doing something. Start in your home with your *next generation.* Groom them for success. Many are fooled into believing that they are helpless, powerless, and without the right connections to make a difference. *But doing nothing is not going to fix it!*

Look at how one person can make a difference: Nana recently wrote, "My husband and I are listening, watching, and telling everyone we know about *Grooming the Next Generation for Success.* Our desire is to use this training to impact the lives of our two married daughters and our ten grandchildren, as much as possible.

"Just this week, I took my grandsons, ages 10 and 5, to the library. As we were passing behind a cluster of computer stations, I caught a glimpse of something that I wasn't sure of and hurriedly walked the boys upstairs to the children's section. My heart was pounding, and I had to go back down to confirm what I thought I might have seen. I stood a distance away, but close enough to see that a man was watching pornography right there in the open where anyone—any child— could see. Angered and shaken to the core, I quickly pointed him out to one of the librarians, and she said she would take care of it. Later she came up to the children's section to inform me that according to Federal Law, they could do nothing about it other than ask him to move to a not-so-conspicuous computer station. We left the library."

This is the type of proaction we are referring to—the courage to address what's wrong and then do something about it. One person can make a difference.

I know that your heart's desire is to design your children's lives for success; otherwise you wouldn't be reading this book. If the method you're currently using is accomplishing the exact opposite, then correct it now while you still have the greatest influence over your children. After all, who wants to intentionally raise another Hitler or Manson? Who wants to raise juvenile delinquents or criminals? Who wants to raise average, mediocre citizens who accept the status quo when the sky is actually the limit? If you don't get them off the wrong path now, you may be intentionally setting them up for a very unsuccessful future.

CHAPTER I

OUR STORY

In many ways, our children are more privileged than we ever were because neither of us was raised in the kind of home we have established for our children, and neither of us knew what it was like to live in a healthy, functional environment like we have today.

MY HUSBAND, HANS

Although Hans's mother did her best to raise her two sons on the Big Island of Hawaii, some of her choices made things hard on all of them. Welfare, food stamps, and lack of housing were the norm for them while growing up. Because of their financial troubles, the young boys worked to bring in extra money—at eight and six years of age.

When Hans was in the third grade and his brother was in kindergarten, they would pick flowers off of trees, make leis, and sell them to tourists after school and on weekends. Sometimes they would dive off the pier to find coins just to have enough money for dinner. Hans's mother was a boat captain, and unfortunately eating at McDonald's was often the only choice when living with her, which was not often because she couldn't afford to maintain a home.

There were times when she would leave for two weeks at a time on a charter, and he and his brother would have to fend for themselves. At other times, they would be sent to stay with their grandparents or friends, or wherever they could lay their heads. Hans has memories of living on a lanai as a young kid and sleeping on a spring mattress with a sheet covering him.

Since Hans was raised without a father, he didn't know how to be a father or a husband. What he did know, though, was that he had an absolute resentment of his family's extreme poverty, which prompted his decision to never be poor again. He made this decision at a very young age, and as a result worked many jobs before the age of 18.

At the time we met, Hans was an 18-year-old commercial diver looking to make extra money. He'd been on his own supporting himself financially since age 12. In fact, he even supported his mother financially during a couple of occasions when she moved in with him. The lures of determining his own future and being financially independent led him to an interview with my company. After coming on board, he attended the debut of my very first seminar, First Steps to Success, in Kona on the Big Island. Shortly afterward, we left Hawaii for California to expand our operation.

ME

My family was on welfare until I was 12. My dad, who raised me from the age of 6 months, was very lazy, extremely angry, and physically abusive. (For 17½ years, I was misled into believing that he was my biological father.) He would beat the snot out of my mother, me, and my two sisters. So my motivation for success was to be nothing like my parents. I just wanted to be free of them and have a normal, functional life. My motivation for success had nothing to do with money.

After my mom broke her neck when I was 11, I became the caretaker for the family. I gave her showers, changed her bedpans, diapers, and dressed her. When I was 14, she got a huge financial settlement. What that did was bring in more expensive drugs, more chaos, more nonsense, and more neglect. So *I hated money.*

But Mom's courage, determination, and persistence was remarkable. She went from living in a bed completely paralyzed from her neck down, to moving an electric wheelchair with her chin. Within five years of her injury, she worked herself into a regular wheelchair, a walker, then a cane, and finally, to riding horses, taking trips on airplanes, and being able to care for herself again. My mother refused to give up, and I was able to witness my first miracle.

My parents took my sisters and me out of public school and placed us into a Christian school. It wasn't because they were converting; it was in hopes of preventing us from unwed pregnancies. This proved to be one of the best things that they ever did for me. The training I received at that Christian school resulted in me receiving Christ as my Lord and Savior at the age of 13. I met Him and He was my *everything* at that time—my Savior, my Safe Place, my Refuge, and my Comforter.

I was molested from the time I was three. At 16, I moved out of the house because I hated the man I called "Dad" who started violating me when I was 12. My mother was doing nothing about it, so I moved. Understand that my parents would be snorting cocaine, smoking weed, taking hundreds of pills, and partying all night long. All I wanted was to do what was right.

All kinds of hostility lived in my childhood home: from being kicked across the room by my father, to watching my mother receive black eyes and bloody noses, even during her years recovering from paralysis. The mental anguish and the physical and emotional pain and suffering I endured during my childhood were horrible.

My sisters grew up in the same house as I did, but their reaction to the abuse was different from mine. They stole my parents' drugs and wound up drug addicts themselves. One sister has been in and out of jail for the last 20 years and the other one is dead. She died from a drug overdose at 21 after doing a drug run for my parents. (Isn't that something? Here were three girls growing up in the same house, seeing and experiencing similar things, yet making different decisions and having different outcomes.)

Making a mistake with the deacon's son (my boyfriend of almost four years who constantly badgered me to have sex), altered my life. I was a senior in high school, living on my own with numerous college scholarships to play basketball, and I found myself pregnant at the age of 17. I soon dropped out of school in order to support myself and my soon-coming baby.

My boyfriend was furious at the news and demanded that I get an abortion. I refused. Then he and his parents pressured me for four months to give the baby up for adoption. I refused. The hypocrisy and condemnation I received from people in my church was harsh, even considering that two in church leadership had illicit pasts.

MASSIVE IDENTITY CRISIS

It was also during this time that I found out I was adopted. When I was three months pregnant with Kristina, my aunt told me that I was adopted by my dad. This news was earth-shattering. My whole life seemed a mess. I had suffered from Mom and Dad's rejection and abandonment for drugs, and then I found out that there was a biological father who had abandoned and rejected me, too. Nothing was ever stable in my life. Everything was always "high drama." I had been totally and deliberately misled by my parents, which caused a massive identity crisis.

During my childhood I was told that I was named after Dan, the man who raised me and whom I called Dad. This seemed feasible since my name is Danette. They also told me that my dark brown eyes came from Dan's father since I was the only dark-skinned person with brown eyes in my immediate family. My sisters were blond with fair skin, and everyone either had green or blue eyes. But in actuality, I was this little Nicaraguan kid who was six months old when Dan came into our lives. It's amazing because it never even dawned on me that I had been lied to even though I was so different from them.

I even bought the lie that my mother was a virgin on her wedding night. Why not? I had no reason not to believe her. It was when my grandmother threatened to tell me the truth while we were still living in Los Angeles that my parents quickly moved us to Northern California.

There is so much stuff I could say about that confusing time in my life, but I'll limit it to this. After all those months of consistent pressure to give up my baby for adoption, I did the most regretful and heartbreaking thing in my life—I released Kristina for adoption.

During that time, I explored various paths to self-improvement and spiritual enlightenment, including Eastern mysticism and the whole metaphysical thing, only to come away with misguided beliefs, a harmful spirituality, a disappointed heart, and a naïve approach to life.

At 18, I met my biological dad, and we've since established an awesome relationship. Everything has been restored; in fact, he even walked me down the aisle when Hans and I recommitted our wedding vows a couple of years ago.

I look at the kind of mother that I am today, and I am totally thankful that our home is the absolute opposite of the home in which I was raised. When I say this, please do not think that I'm bragging about myself. Rather, I am totally boasting in God who rescued me from my past, blessed me with an awesome family, and surrounded me with great people, great clients, and great friends who have made a massive impact on my life. Gone forever are the daily verbal and physical assaults from a drug-addicted father who was pathetically enabled by an indifferent, drug-addicted mother.

How I ended up in Hawaii, 3,000 miles away from home, is another long story, so I'll just give you the highlights. When I was

21, I eloped with a man I barely knew after being with him for seven days. We eventually moved to Hawaii. For me, it seemed like a fairy tale come true. I'd married a charming prince and had moved to a beautiful place to live life happily ever after. Up until that point, my life had been a roller-coaster ride of personal disappointments, few shining moments, and many painful memories.

DECEIVED AND DEPRESSED

At 18, I left my hometown and all the painful memories and people to start a new life. At 19, I was introduced to the concept of becoming an entrepreneur, something I knew nothing about. After attending several classes given by successful, multimillionaire business owners, I figured that even if I failed to produce their income by 90 percent, and even if it took me 20 years to learn how to get good at it, I would still be doing better being self-employed than if I stayed at JCPenney's.

I found a product to market, and I was in business. After six months of absolute failure and living off of my credit cards, it was apparent that being in business was much harder than I thought it would be. I began looking for people who were succeeding and invested in educating myself about how to succeed in business. I spent thousands of dollars and learned much. In fact, I stopped losing money and within a few months realized incomes of over $20,000 a month. I was amazed.

I felt that I had finally arrived. For the first time in my life, I had money, confidence, and celebrity-star status. People had actually sought me out to see what they could learn from me—from me. Earlier that year while at a training event in Los Angeles, I received numerous accolades as the top-earning sales rep for a business I'd operated. One of the attendees asked if he could pick my brain for some business tips. He looked like a movie star, was incredibly charming, and made me feel wanted, appreciated, and important. We spent the following week together, and at the end of that week, got married after I had fallen head-over-heels for him.

This proved to be a big mistake. Within four months, the man I married deserted me for another woman and drained my bank account. I was left with a $35,000 debt and exactly $2.03 to my name. I felt what it was to be completely devastated, totally abandoned, hopelessly confused, and very, very scared. Evicted from my house shortly afterward, everything I owned was packed into my tiny car. I found myself parked on a beach, showering in public facilities, not knowing where I was going to sleep or where my next meal was coming from.

It was an absolutely devastating and humiliating time. To make matters worse, my business on the mainland had also been embezzled at the very same time. Everything had been lost—my savings, my friends, my dignity, but worst of all, my dreams. I had no vision, and that was a dangerous place to be. Feeling blindsided and confused, I drifted around in a total daze. I found myself hanging out at a beach with a handful of people I didn't know, which provided a diversion from my loneliness and a convenient escape from despair. The beach was a favorite spot for people wanting to avoid the realities of life. They shared with me their carefree spirits, invited me into their careless lifestyle, and shared with me their means of escape—marijuana. Soon, this became my daily routine. I would hang out at the beach, toke out on weed, and drift along for another day.

During this time, I managed to get a job as a cocktail waitress. But even then, I still smoked pot upon awaking each morning since work didn't start until 3 o'clock in the afternoon. The first two weeks as a waitress, I received unpaid training. I survived day-to-day, with no direction, hope, or clue about what I was going to do.

After hitting rock-bottom—homeless, living out of my car, depressed, contemplating suicide, and 50 pounds overweight, I had a defining moment. This is when I came face-to-face with my reality and stood at the crossroads of my life.

DEFINING MOMENT

It was Christmas Eve and I was wasted. Something I swore I would never do, I did that night—that was snorting cocaine. When I left my parents' home several years earlier, I had sworn to myself that I would never be like them and that I would never use drugs, especially cocaine. But there I was, facing the same demons that tormented my family, stole my innocence, and destroyed my childhood. The next thing I remember is being on the beach the following day and having this powerful craving for more cocaine. The hunger for it consumed me, and I became frustrated because I couldn't find any.

Feeling like I was hitting a brick wall, I waded out into the tide. A wave approached, and as it was about to break, I dove under it. When I came up, a change swept over me and removed the intense craving I had moments before. I was clear-headed. Then I heard a voice say, *"Pick up your mat and walk."*

The day after this defining moment, I became completely focused with no more whining, crying the blues, complaining, or pity parties. I was still waitressing full-time, but from the trunk of my car and using a payphone booth, I started licensing a weight-loss product from a manufacturer. Using these meager resources, within the first 45 days, I made $18,000. Needless to say, I quit waitressing at that point. I then went on to make a quarter-of-a-million dollars by the end of my first year and my first million at the end of my second year. It's amazing what can be accomplished with a burning desire to succeed. I am so thankful that I have never been homeless since.

As my business grew, so did my reputation as a marketing professional. This is when I conducted my first seminar called *First Steps to*

Success. One weekend each month, I taught other entrepreneurs successful business skills. Attendance at these training seminars expanded rapidly, and it was then that I decided to contact a nutritional laboratory to custom-manufacture products under a private label and start my own health and nutrition company.

The following year, I made my first million, and within two years, I became the owner and president of two multi-million dollar companies—all of this by the age of 23. In 1996, I sold my health and nutrition company and focused my efforts on my training company. Since then I have made millions of dollars building various companies and helping other people succeed financially through our training company.

US

Hans and I have worked together as a team from almost the very beginning of this business venture. Since then, we have had outrageous success—as well as devastating hardships. Each experience has made us who we are today.

Today we have so much to be thankful for. I'm thankful for a loving, faithful husband, a great family, five wonderful children, and an awesome profession as an author, speaker, business trainer, and coach. My life has been blessed in more ways than I ever dreamed possible. I shudder to think where I might have ended up if I had taken a wrong turn at the crossroads of my life and missed the defining moment that positively changed my life forever.

The path I took led me to Hans, my children, and wealth...and it absolutely led me straight back to God and to numerous miracles. The miracle of my daughter Kristina returning into my life when she was 14 was major. How we both searched for each other at the same time and were miraculously reunited is the subject for another book. The manipulation that stole her from me, the lies that were told about me, and the abuse she personally suffered at the hands of her adoptive parents has all been rectified.

Two people from two different families and two different areas ended up having several things in common. Both of us had a childhood that no one in their right minds would want. We weren't groomed to be successful as children or taught by our parents how to become millionaires. No one in our families had achieved that measure of success, and yet both of us became millionaires in our 20s and are multi-millionaires today.

Let us assure you: There is hope available for you if you find yourself in the dire predicaments we were in. Our past backgrounds did not represent our present or future realities. Likewise, your past does not have to equal your present or your future, either. As long as you are still breathing, it's not too late to implement the changes required to *groom your next generation for success.*

CHAPTER 2

WHY GROOM THE NEXT GENERATION?

*Train a child in the way that he should go, and
when he is old he will not turn from it.*

—PROVERBS 22:6

Today, mass murderers and criminals of every kind are common-place in our nation and world. Just read any newspaper or watch any newscast on any given day; crimes of this magnitude are happening somewhere on this planet. Behind the scenes, a story seldom told is taking place—the humiliation, shame, and grief of parents enduring the despicable crimes of their children. Believe you me, after parents comprehend the full extent of the havoc their adult children have wreaked in the lives of others, joy is not the emotion that they experience. After all, who in their right mind would want to see their children go down in history with a badge of dishonor, disgust, and disdain? And who really wants to shoulder the blame for raising children like that? Whether you're in agreement or not, in most cases some of the blame rests with the parents or with others who have influenced them.

In this book I share some useful strategies for parents, teachers, youth leaders, aunts, uncles, and everyone with young people around them. If you fall into this category, this will give you confident assurance in knowing that you did your absolute best in raising your children, grandkids, nieces, nephews, students, etc. Then you'll be able to say, "I did the very best that I could. I gave it my best shot; now it's up to my children to do the rest." No regrets are definitely better than having the opposite be true.

We don't control the actions of our children when they become adults, but while they are young, we can lay a strong foundation offering them strong decision-making skills to confront any situation wisely.

WHO IS IN YOUR HOME?

To begin, let me ask these questions: Who is in your home, and what kind of changes need to happen within *you* so that your *next generation* can emerge unscathed as much as is possible? (Grandparents, aunts, uncles, and godparents, this question also applies to you.)

The Answers: The future is in your home, and the opportunity to change the future lives in your home. And if you interact with the *next generation* as part of your job or profession (teachers, social workers, probation officers, nurses, etc.), the future and the opportunity to change the future is in your office. That means those in the medical profession, education, social work, or religious settings can also use and apply this content. Whether children are living with you in your home or not is not the issue. This is what I know, *every child who comes in contact with you is the future of this world, and yours is an awesome responsibility to impact them successfully.*

The fact that you have the opportunity to change the course your child is heading on is a great responsibility and one that should not be taken lightly. Since you have the authority, the opportunity, and the responsibility, all you need is the right motivation and skills to successfully accomplish this.

So again, who's in the palm of your hands? Who's in your home or within easy reach? Could it be a future professional athlete, a coach, a businessman or a businesswoman, a scientist, an inventor, an actor or actress, a famous celebrity? Could it be another Mother Teresa, a preacher, a teacher, a prophet, the president of a nation, or a CEO of a powerful corporation? What about a future entrepreneur, politician, judge, prime minister, mayor, governor, doctor, or lawyer? I guarantee you, the future leader of a country is being birthed and trained right now somewhere on this planet. The point is that it could be your child.

Your child could also become a full-time, loving housewife or a highly moral and qualified mechanic. If they're happy and content with their lot in life, that's all that matters. That is success for them. Success is not determined by the size of your bank account or your status in life. Success is different for each person. When you can define what it is for you, it will have far greater value than the mainstream idea of success.

So do you understand who is in your home and under your direct influence? Begin to see your children in the future tense instead of the present reality. View them as the potential young men and women that they will eventually become. Keep in mind also that our time and the window of opportunity to effect changes in them are short. Time marches on.

Now consider the answers to these questions to determine your level of commitment and motivation to those under your influence:

- How do you want them to lead and influence others?

- What outcome are you seeking for yourself: sadness, grief, gladness, or joy?

- Do you want to confidently know now who and what you're raising?

- Will you work diligently with the spirit of excellence to equip them now?

If your desire is for your children to wildly succeed and accomplish even more than you have, your desire is in the right place. That's the way it's supposed to be. We're supposed to leave them a legacy and make life easier, not harder, for them. We're supposed to pass on blessings rather than curses so that our bloodline can build on our successes and expand into greater and newer territories. We're to carve out a direction for them that allows blessings to reign in their lives so that they may be a blessing to others.

I had curses passed down from my family—generational curses. My family hated God; they were alcoholics, drug addicts, and greedy people (some of whom even sued each other). Murder is in my bloodline; so are incest, molestation, and rape. I had such a wonderful bloodline that my grandmother was even a mistress in the Mafia. This was the heritage that my family gave me.

Everyone has some negative legacy that was passed down from previous generations, but you can absolutely take a stand and prevent it from being passed on any further. That's what we've done with our children, and so can you.

THE SAD REALITY

Unfortunately, we're living in a generation where directing our children to be blessed and be blessings is not reality. The sad reality, in my humble opinion, is that we are the first generation overall where this trend has reversed. Our generation is far worse off than our parents' generation financially, emotionally, mentally, physically, and spiritually. I could be wrong, but this is my assessment after taking an honest look around.

According to a 2008 report, although the abortion rate is now at its lowest level since 1974, the number of abortions in the United States is staggering—1.2 million in 2005, and similar numbers in years before and after![1] This means that on average there are between 3,300-3,700 abortions performed every day of the year in our country.

The divorce rate and the rate of unmarried people choosing a single lifestyle because of the ill effects they were subjected to as children has skyrocketed. Our nation is in the midst of a financial crisis, a health crisis, wars, and rumors of wars.

So, honestly, would you agree that the way life is going now is a bit scary? Would you be honest enough to say that within the last 50 years many huge transformations have taken place in our society that have not necessarily been beneficial? Enormous changes have occurred, and I guarantee you, more is on the horizon. These changes began in our parents' generation, and generation after generation has followed that decline. (I'm sorry to bring you the bad news, but I promise to bring some good news later.)

It's time to step up and pull together in unity for the sake of the *next generation* in our homes, in our schools, and in our society. There has never been a more desperate time or cry as is in our nation today.

We live in a time when there is so much corruption that we don't even know what goodness and righteousness look like anymore. We live in a time when righteousness is called "evil" and evil is acceptable. We also live in a time when political correctness takes a higher priority over biblical correctness. It seems that our personal morality is being used as a yardstick to measure our morality against someone else's immorality.

I hope and pray that your eyes are opened in case you've compromised some places in your life and fallen victim into that trap. My friend, I have to tell you that there are traps on every corner, but there is also a God who is faithful to His Word. If you commit your ways to Him, He will strengthen and bring you through every trap and snare. He will open your eyes to the evil that is so pervasive in our culture in order for you to stand firmly against it, fighting for what is right, noble, pure, and praiseworthy. Are you willing to stand?

One home at a time...this is my passion.

ANOTHER PASSION

Another reason for my passion is that I believe there is a clear plan of evil to *kill the seed*. This is not a new plan, but it is definitely an evil one. If you look back to the time of Moses, Pharaoh made a declaration to murder all Israeli male babies at birth. (See Exodus 1:16.) The same happened when Jesus was born. King Herod executed all babies aged two years and under. He single-handedly destroyed the *next generation* of the male seed. (See Matthew 2:16.)

As it was then, so it is today. In fact, in some places, it is considered good to destroy the seed.

I just read a story that brought tears to my eyes and a passion through me. Eight-year-old girls in Thailand are sold into sex slavery on a regular basis. They're put in brothels and required to turn ten to twenty sex trades a day. When these babies themselves are impregnated, the seed/child is aborted, and they are forced into bed with another man two hours later. That is killing the seed. Not just the aborted baby, but the 8-10-12-year-old *seed* whose life has been tragically destroyed. In another life, she would have been a respectable mother raising her children within an honorable marriage. But that was robbed from her and replaced with the nightmare of being beaten, raped, and forced to have sex with as many as twenty men a day.

Oh, that's terrible for Thailand, you're thinking, but what about Jamaica where 8-year-old boys are being sold into sex slavery for the pleasure of rich, male tourists? Predominantly American and European men are buying an hour of sex from little boys at several hotels. Blind eyes are being turned away from the whole ugly affair. (These hotels are supposedly for adults only because they have a fully nude beach as part of the amenities.)

I verified this information with two different cab drivers when I was in Jamaica:

"What about the so-and-so hotel?" I asked.

"Oh, you don't want to hear about *dat!*"

"I do. Tell me about it."

Independently, each cab driver disclosed information about the huge sex trade for young boys in Jamaica. Recruiters solicit these boys from parents who can't afford to feed their families, so they offer their boys for food. That's exactly how the sex trade in Thailand operates. Some daughters are sold because of hunger, while others are sold for luxuries, like TVs. After these girls are brought to the brothel, their parents never see them again.

This happens in the United States as well. Young children are being sold into slavery every year in the United States, according to the article, "Money and Fear, An Underground Form of Slavery." According to the Department of Justice, 400,000 young children and teens in the U.S. are lured into prostitution annually.[2]

Can you see that this evil plan, after all this time, has not changed? It has continued to *steal, kill, and destroy,* and the target is *your* seed. The target is the *next generation.* This evil plan is after our seed today more than ever before.

It's happening worldwide; if you don't believe that the seed is the target, you're simply in denial. Realize that even our government is attacking the seed in the womb. Our seed is in serious danger and being killed to the tune of millions. Check the latest abortion statistics.

If you call yourself a Christian and you believe that abortion is not bad or that a fetus is not a baby until after birth, 50 percent of the Christian population shares your opinion. But in my opinion, this just proves that you haven't read your Bible cover-to-cover.

Try this story on for size. Genesis 25:21-24 names Rebecca as the first woman to initiate having a conversation with the Lord, and He responded. (In regard to speaking to God after He first spoke to them, Eve was the first female recorded in Scripture, Sarah the second, and Hagar the third.)[3]

> [Rebecca] *said, "Why is this happening to me?" So she went to inquire of the Lord. The Lord said to her, "Two nations are in your womb, and two peoples from within you will be separated; one people will be stronger than the other, and the older will serve the younger." When the time came for her to give birth, there were twin boys in her womb* (Genesis 25:22-24).

The Bible says twin boys, two nations, and two peoples were in her womb. So if you still think that a fetus is not a baby until after birth, then you've just admitted:

1. That you've not read or understood the Book of Genesis, or

2. That you've not personally read the Bible cover-to-cover, or

3. You're trusting the pastor or a leader behind the pulpit to teach you the Word of God, or

4. You're allowing the media to desensitize you.

I'll give you the benefit of the doubt. The media has desensitized you, and your church leadership has not contradicted this opinion. Church leaders are under restriction and have been silenced on this subject. They've signed a document called a 501C3 that effectively prevents them from discussing political issues, such as abortion, if they want to continue collecting offerings from their congregation. So *of course* you didn't realize that a fetus in a womb is actually a baby.

According to "Abortion No," there are about 3,700 abortions a day in our country. What was the calling for all of those kids? What was their calling especially given the account of a pregnant woman in Genesis who carried twins (two nations)?

It's reported that the abortion rate is exactly the same in the Church as it is outside of the Church.[4] The truth is that there is no moral compass in or out of the Church. According to Barna Research, morality continues to decay within the Church. Of the ten moral behaviors evaluated, a majority of Americans believed gambling (61%), cohabitation (60%), and sexual fantasies (59%) were acceptable. Nearly half of the adult population felt that having an abortion (45%) and having a sexual relationship with someone of the opposite sex other than their spouse (42%) were morally acceptable. About one-third of the population gave the stamp of approval to pornography (38%). The activity that garnered the least support was using non-prescription drugs (17%).[5]

With this type of climate in and out of the Church, it's small wonder that our children have not been groomed to honor purity. They have no idea about "saving themselves until marriage" or being "unblemished." They are clueless, and it looks like some parents are, too.

Could it be that some of us who went down the same road feel unqualified to speak to youth about purity? Do we think that we don't have the voice to speak into their lives? *I screwed up, so I don't have the right to tell them to do what I didn't do.* Or is pride so much of an issue that we must hide our past mistakes to preserve our reputations? That, my friend, is pride. That is not allowing God to get the glory for what He has walked you through in order that someone else can benefit from your mistakes.

Throughout the whole Bible, He has repeatedly said, "Don't forget what I've brought you through" and *"teach the children the way that they should go."* He did not say to leave out your mistakes, otherwise the Bible would be filled with happy, hunky-dory stories—and it is not. It's filled with blood, guts, rape, thievery, and murder.

We have His Word now because it was written, taught, and passed from one generation to the next. God clearly wanted human mistakes as well as testimonies of His divine power brought forth to prevent His children from making the same mistakes as their forefathers.

Today we have a generation of parents with big egos who have made mistakes in the past and are attempting to hide the truth from their children (and everyone else).

Get over yourself, already! Confess it and equip your children to learn from your mistakes. You have the right, the authority, and the qualifications to do so. Since you have endured the pain and the suffering, this gives you the right to help prevent your children and others from doing the same thing. Overcoming your sufferings has qualified you; and if you speak from a loving viewpoint and not as a dictator, they will hear you. (Make sure that they understand that your only motive is to protect and to prevent them from going down the same road as you.)

Don't lie to them! Remember, my mom lied to me my entire childhood, saying among other things that she was a virgin on her wedding night. The fact is that she didn't marry Dan until I was 8, and by their wedding night, my other two sisters had already been born. Putting us in a Christian school for pregnancy prevention was their motive, but it was also a way to protect their lies. But the cover-up didn't work. I still got pregnant and the truth about my mom's teen pregnancy eventually came out.

ENDNOTES

1. Guttmacher Institute; http://www.guttmacher.org/media/nr/2008/01/17/index.html (accessed July 3, 2009).

2. Andrea Laurita, "Money and Fear, An Underground Form of Slavery"; http://www.multnomah.edu/VOICE/0504/0504cover2.html (accessed July 3, 2009).

3. Genesis 3:13, 18:10-15, 21:17.

4. www.abortionno.org/Resorces/fastfacts.html

5. www.crossroad.to/charts/church-statistics.html

CHAPTER 3

THE WAKE-UP CALL

He who works his land will have abundant food,
but the one who chases fantasies will have his fill
of poverty.

—**Proverbs 28:19**

This is *your* wake-up call. Our generation needs to rise up and declare, "Hands off! Not my seed, and not on my watch! We will raise the remnant that will succeed and change the future." This great nation, the "land of the free and the home of the brave" was established by a few, by a remnant, by a seed, and that's what it will take to change the course and direction of the *next generation* and our nation. If we stand together, this generation's course can be corrected and their destinies fulfilled beyond our wildest imaginations.

As a whole, we've become desensitized and have lowered our moral standards. We've become numb to the negative effects of our self-absorbed society. We've ignorantly accepted complacency and the notion *that evil is good and acceptable*. **We are asleep and need a wake-up call!**

As parents, you are the chief influencers in your children's lives. Even if they appear not to be listening to you, they are. You have to take a stand and do your part.

Many adults are going through inner healing due to the absence or abuse of their past chief influencers. Some have already completed the process. But the fact remains—parents are the chief influencers and the lack of parental support has a lingering effect on children, even after they become adults. So whether you feel like you have the respect of your children or not, trust me, you have the *influence* and it extends over every kid that you are willing to sow encouragement and vision into. Your influence extends to every kid you are willing to gird and groom in the right direction.

Do not be deceived; every parent has influence over their kids. Don't feel helpless and think: *Oh, there's no hope. They're not going to listen! It's not going to work, so why even try?*

Trust me; they will listen because God fulfills His Word and His promises. He promises that if we do our part, He will do His. *"Train a child in the way he should go, and when he is old he will not turn from it"* (Proverbs 22:6).

THE DIFFERENCE BETWEEN 98 PERCENT AND 2 PERCENT

At home with our kids and at the onset of our training seminars, I always establish the distinction between two populations—2 percent versus 98 percent of the population. The statistics are scary. They affirm that the vast majority of people (98 percent) reach the end of their lives having not accomplished their original goals. In other words, by the age of 65, this population is dead or dead broke. But the rest of the population (2 percent) is doing financially well at the same age.

I have personally spent years examining and reading studies from other researchers on these two diverse populations. The first study conducted was in the 1930s. Its goal was to distinguish differences between those who became millionaires and those who had struggled financially and otherwise their entire lives.

These studies revealed that there is always a small remnant of people who will do what it takes to succeed in every area of their lives. This is the 2 percent. The vast majority of people won't do what it takes to succeed. The truth of this concept can be seen in Olympic athletes versus other athletes and across the board in every sector. In fact, in marriages and parenting, only a few will do what it takes to succeed by acquiring the needed skill sets.

So I celebrate you right now for reading this book. Obviously, you're part of the remnant that God awoke because He is the only One who can. You are the one saying, "Hello! I need some help. I don't want to just raise kids; I want to raise successful kids, kids who will have a better life and a better shot than I ever had."

As part of the remnant, let me welcome and encourage you. We will go through the journey together, and if you decide to join us at one of our live events, then you will meet a whole bunch of other people just like you. You are not alone. There are hundreds of thousands of people who are part of the 2 percent crowd desiring something greater than the status quo.

I've raised my kids on the concept of 98 and 2, and it helps tremendously when they come home asking for a game or toy that their friends have, such as a Nintendo, for example. Our answer is always this, "That's great for them; however, that's not necessarily going to be best for your present or your future. We choose to make wise choices based on what 2 percent of the population would do instead of what everybody else is doing."

I essentially teach my kids and clients to *find out what everybody else is doing, and then, do the exact opposite*. If everybody else is after the Nintendo, then we do the exact opposite. (We have never had or bought a Nintendo.) If everybody else has cable—we don't. If teenage girls shop at the malls every weekend on Mom and Dad's credit cards, my girls won't! If everyone else's boys are involved in two or three different sport activities and other extracurricular lessons at the same time—not our boys!

Find out what the vast majority of the population is doing and go in the opposite direction. If you do, there's a pretty good chance you will succeed in your endeavors.

Just look at the general population and ask yourself, *Are they succeeding?* On the surface they may look like they are successful, but when you get underneath the surface, there lies the truth. Typically found are broken-hearted, messed-up, lost, and foolish people on the path of self-destruction. Their lives are controlled by debt because they can't say no to themselves or to their children; and they are being led by the fear of man, which is the fear of what others will think of them.

This is a captive, not a free person. Anyone who is afraid of what others think is in captivity. This type of parent lives vicariously through their children and brings attention to the fact that their son is attending Harvard or wherever. They boast in the achievements of their children.

"Good for you," is my response. "Nice bill you have there."

Why do we feel pressed to make our kids go to college? Are we just trying to look good, or is it really best for the child? Do your kids even know what they really want to do with their lives, or are we pressing them to do certain things so we can boast?

When we really get below the surface, the truth will come out. What I've seen from working with hundreds of thousands of people is that they are reaching for something they don't really want. When they sit down and ask themselves, *"Why are my kids in five or six activities that are stressing them and me out? There's no family time; do I just want to look good on the outside?"*

Why do we buy certain types of cars or clothes? In my humble opinion, it's all captivity—the way 98 percent of the population lives. Right now, only a remnant can hear me, so if you haven't thrown this book on the floor yet, then you're obviously called to be different and set apart. It's part of the grand design. You've been purposely designed to be different and set apart.

THE DESENSITIZING PROCESS

Some of us have compromised and have fallen in line with the status quo. We are not living under the grand design to be different and set apart. As I stated before, we have lowered our moral standards and have become desensitized.

How have we become *desensitized*? How has this happened?

In the business community, I teach a simple process titled *Expose, Involve, and Advance.* A tremendous number of our clients have earned 6-figure incomes on a part-time or full-time basis, and some have even gone on to make millions of dollars by using this 3-step process. Other businesses have also used this model successfully— including the Internet pornography business. It's a strategy that has been proven successful.

In regard to pornography, studies that I have come across say that 95 percent of all children have been exposed. That means that they have actually seen pornography with their eyes.

I don't believe that a kid would intentionally look for porn until after the first exposure. It could occur accidentally while playing a game, walking by a computer in a library, or talking to a friend on the Internet. Bam! A pop-up appears exposing innocent kids and leading them to other websites (the involvement stage) that eventually succeeds in hooking them (the advancement stage). They enter the involvement stage by clicking one link to the next. The next time they're on the Internet—click!—they are intentionally looking for pornography, instantly crossing over into the advancement stage of the 3-part process. Now, they are sucked up into a disgusting, horrifying addiction and lured into increasingly grosser sites.

As far as *soft* porn goes, every child has been exposed just by glancing at magazine covers. These days, simply standing in a grocery checkout line allows exposure.

Regardless of the statistics, I don't want any child in my household exposed, accidentally or not. So I talk to them and monitor their activities regularly, even when we are at the grocery store or they are on the Internet. (I suggest that you do the same thing because if your kids have been exposed, something has to be done about it simply because of what it leads to.)

According to psychologists Michele Ybarra, PhD, and Kimberly Mitchell, PhD, nearly 90 percent or more of children between the ages of 14 and older have access to the Internet. These kids are intentionally looking for porn, which is the end result of an accidental exposure. In other words, they are hooked.

Dr. Ybarra is president of Internet Solutions for Kids, Inc. and is a recognized researcher in Internet-related health issues for young people. Dr. Mitchell is a research assistant professor of psychology at the Crimes against Children Research Center at the University of New Hampshire. Using data from the Youth Internet Safety Survey (a nationally representative, cross-sectional telephone survey of 1,501 children and adolescents between the ages of 10 to 17), they've identified characteristics associated with self-reported, pornography-seeking behavior on the Internet and through traditional methods, like magazines.

"Children under the age of 14 who have intentionally looked at pornography are more likely to report traditional exposures, such as magazines or movies. Those who report intentional exposure to pornography, irrespective of source, are significantly more likely to cross-sectionally report delinquent behavior and substance use in the previous year. Further, online seekers versus offline seekers are more likely to report clinical features associated with depression and lower levels of emotional bonding with their caregiver."[1]

Their study was based on those who intentionally looked for porn. Look at the statistics for *unintentional* exposure. Safe Families, Keeping Children Safe Online, writes "that 9 out of 10 children aged between the ages of 8 and 16 have viewed pornography on the Internet, in most cases unintentionally.[2]

If your children watch television, 100 percent of them have been exposed to pornography. Remember the great protest against the "King of Rock and Roll" several generations ago? Television stations restricted displaying Elvis' dance movements from the waist down. But today your children regularly look at cartoon images on Saturday mornings filled with lust and seduction, and the media executives condone it.

Our family stopped watching television eight years ago after a station that we thought was family-safe aired a commercial at 7:30 on a Saturday morning for the movie *American Pie*. It just so happened, I walked past the TV set at the same moment an actress stripped. I couldn't believe it. A girl's bikini top—boom! As soon as she was exposed, the camera scanned away, but you know what they're seeing and thinking. Then—boom—just as quickly, two people were making out. This is what our little girl (9) and young boys (7, 5, and 3) were being exposed to from an approved station and an approved show.

Do I have censorship over the commercials airing at 7:30 in the morning? Who would make a decision to program an advertisement or movie preview of a girl removing a bikini top in front of our young children? What lesson is that teaching them and how is the media grooming them? Sex out of marriage is OK.

It's hard nowadays to even find a television show without a boyfriend and girlfriend living together. What does that scenario promote to our children? What way of life is that teaching them to accept? It teaches that sex out of marriage is OK.

Immorality is in the land. Morality is considered odd and politically incorrect. We live in a time when evil is considered good and good is considered evil. We are living in a time when our moral compasses are programmed to accept harmful and hurtful information. Not only is this affecting us, but also the *next generation.* Small wonder our teens are having abortions, virgins are scarce, and morality is non-existent. We have become desensitized, my friend, and have easily accepted the exposure to seduction and lust through *soft* porn on television and smut magazines in the supermarket checkout aisle.

The media understands well the process of desensitizing. When you constantly allow streams of images, messages, and items into your home via Internet, radio, print, and television, the desensitizing process begins.

Consider the seductive voices and content on Saturday morning cartoons. Why does Jessica Rabbit have an hourglass figure for entertaining 8 and 10-year-old boys, and what is she teaching little girls? Boys are being taught to desire that kind of woman when they grow up. Little girls are learning how to dress seductively and talk in a manner that will capture male attention. The end result is immorality, teen pregnancy, molestation, or rape.

If you've been to a dance studio or a dance recital at one time or another, you've seen how little girls are taught to dance. If you've ever been to a studio that teaches gymnastics, jazz, or tap, then you've seen that the majority of these studios teach 3, 4, and 5-year-old girls how to move seductively. They dress them in alluring costumes and train them to move their bodies in a sexy manner, just like Jessica Rabbit. The audience applauds and claps and accepts this type of behavior. Then we can't understand why our little girls are being molested.

Child molestation statistics are high, roughly 33 percent of girls and 14 percent of boys are molested before the age of 18, according to the U. S. Justice Department. "In most cases, however, child moles-tation goes unreported. Estimates are that only 35 percent of sexual abuse is reported. Kids can be frightened or embarrassed and many times do not say anything."[3] (I was 3 years old when I was molested the first time.)

For that reason, I've never allowed Arika to join one of those dance studios. I searched all over the San Francisco Bay area looking for studios that did not promote seduction in dance or dress and found none. (I know that there are hundreds of dance studios in the Bay Area, and I was willing to drive the distance for Arika, but I couldn't find one.) Even those classified as "Christian" had seductive dance movements.

Parents, we've sat back and applauded at those recitals long enough. We just go along with it because we own the 98 percent way of thinking. But if you're reading this book, you are not to be part of the 98; you are set to be in the 2 percent. You are part of the remnant that *will* stand up and do what is right, setting the standard for every-body else to follow.

I've had people come to me and say, "Your kids are amazing. How have you done that?" People will say the same to you when you take a stand. If you blend in with everybody else, then you can say what everybody else says. "Oh, that's just kid's stuff." Well, you have fun with that statement. Have fun with your child's molestation and teenage pregnancy, too.

So back to Jessica Rabbit; please tell me why she has that form and speaks in that manner? What is the point of that content? What is the point of her script?

It's all about lust and seduction.

This is also the reason for video games of women fighting in skin-tight hot pants that reveal too much anatomy. What's the point? Can you please tell me why, if this is children's entertainment, Jessica's measurements have to be 40-20-34?

We have become desensitized and have fallen asleep. We are submitting our children to teachings and images that are hurtful and have allowed immorality to increase in our land. We live in a time where evil is considered good; and good (or morality) is considered evil.

My objective is to equip you to make decisions that will limit your children's exposure to immorality in this 3-step process of Expose, Involve, and Advance. Let me show you how this works using the example of pornography.

STEP 1—EXPOSURE

I read a book recently about pornography, and it just blew my mind. A chapter revealed the history and origin of this industry, but what grabbed my attention was the method used to increase pornography after it reached a sales plateau. In order to take sales to a higher level, this multibillion dollar industry decided to target women. When that didn't work, children were the next logical target. Getting children addicted while young became a strategy guaranteeing future returns.

Pornographers literally sat around a table in a boardroom to figure out ways to market their enterprise and increase their revenues. Their answer was to expose your children (and mine) to *soft* porn. By starting this process early in their lives, they would be fully addicted and fully upgraded into the system by the time they were mature enough to have money consistently in their hands. (Appalling, isn't it?)

Expose, Involve, and Advance was the technique used to begin this assault. Innocent children have been hooked through soft exposure to porn—a little dose at a time, beginning with commercials, advertisements, and billboards, then graduating to cartoons, magazines, catalogs, and the Internet.

Billboards—Near the airport in the Bible-belt suburbs of Dallas, do you know what's being advertised? Gigantic billboards of half-naked women promoting gentlemen's clubs. Texas is supposed to be a family-oriented state with Christian morals, right? But what I'm quickly discovering is that kids are not safe anywhere. They are constantly being exposed.

That billboard with a half-naked woman exposes your child to pornography, and we parents just keep on driving, saying nothing, and ignoring its obvious impact. But it is doing something within your little boy and little girl.

"No, sons, that is not the woman you want to be with. No, daughter, that is not the look you want to have." I say this every time we come in contact with similar exposures. I ask them to close their eyes or if I'm not driving, I'll turn around and captivate them by saying, "Guys, look me in the eyes right now and don't take your eyes off of mine. There's a billboard coming up, and I don't want you to look at it. This billboard is trying to expose and tempt you into something that you don't want and never want to become."

Magazines—That partially undressed woman on the magazine cover in the check-out line is also an exposure. So not to have to fix a problem later, I'll equip our boys beforehand when approaching the checkout.

"Boys, we are going to the checkout line and there will be women on magazine covers. These are not the kind of women that you want to put your trust in or spend your life with. They are a trap for seduction and lust. So if you see anything that is displeasing to God and would tempt you in any way, turn that thing around. We'll also help protect every other little boy in this store so that they don't have to be tempted in that way."

"OK, Mom."

Then, we'll turn around every seductive magazine we see while standing in the checkout line. It's about being proactive.

Catalogs—When's the last time you looked at the bra and panty sections in Victoria's Secret or the JCPenney catalog? Believe it or not, that's how the addiction began with many young men. One male client admitted that his hook was the catalog. "I was eight years old and my mom was looking for bras in a catalog. That was my start. As soon as I saw it, I was hooked. I got that catalog and I kept thumbing through it."

It starts with something as innocent sounding as a catalog, but it comes to the house to tempt your little boys to look at things they don't need to be looking at and causes your little girls to think they have to live up to that type of unrealistic standard. This is how the pornography industry is attacking the children in your home, the children in your churches, and the children in your schools; and we allow this exposure to *soft* porn because we're asleep.

I've met and counseled many men and women trapped by an addiction to pornography, which resulted in the loss of families and fortunes. In fact, I have a personal Christian friend going through a sex addiction program right now because he spent $300,000 on pornography in the last two years.

Based on the professional opinions of therapists I've interviewed, pornography is currently the number one addiction in the United States of America. Professionals with PhD degrees who have been counseling for more than 30 and 40 years say that pornography is the greatest epidemic that has ever hit this nation.

Dr. Lavonne Atnip, PhD, a licensed therapist for 35 years, has attended many of our seminars. She said that pornography is far worse than any addiction she'd ever seen. "This is the strongest of all addictions in the last 35 years and has a greater effect than any of the drugs from the 1960s, '70s, and '80s. It's more powerful than crank with the same effect on the brain as crystal methamphetamine."

Dr. Atnip recounted the story of two brothers, aged 6 and 13, who became addicted to Internet pornography. The older brother was surfing the net when a pop-up appeared and hooked him. Afterward, he spent hours every day watching porn until his younger brother caught him and threatened to tell their mother.

"'Don't say a word and I'll show you how to do it,' the older brother bribed.

"So now the 13 and the 6-year-old are going through counseling for Internet pornography, and the youngest one still refuses to give it up."

Does this story shock you? Some of us allow our kids free access to the Internet, and nearly 90 percent of them have already been exposed to it while online. If you study about how powerful Internet porn is on kids, you may want to start making some changes *now*.

We had to. A nice Christian boy, whose parents are very close friends, was trusted to be home-schooled by himself using the Internet. His parents thought he would make the right decisions due to his Christian upbringing. (This was an approved house!) Well, this young man, who is three years older than our son, was exposed to Internet porn at a young age, and he made the unwise decision to expose our son.

We met with the parents and the boys together and brought it all out in the open. Lovingly and without shame, we had our son confess. Today both boys live with clear consciences. Obviously our son is not allowed on anyone else's Internet, and he is grateful for that rule of accountability. He knows it is to help him succeed. The boys are still allowed to visit each other's houses, but when they are together, they have clear boundaries. They will not have Internet access or be unchaperoned when together.

This older boy awakened our son prematurely, which prompted us to have sex talks earlier than planned. Our son's innocence was robbed very early, and just as quickly, it was replaced by a desire that lives inside of him. As a result, our son has had to constantly fight for purity. In thought and action, he's winning the battle, so far.

STEP 2—INVOLVEMENT

Pornographers know what they're doing. They use soft exposure in the beginning, then gradually increase the dosage. Children (as well as adults) begin taking in a little bit more over time. *That's involvement.* Your kids will begin picking up more magazines and watching more cartoon characters with cleavage and sexual content. Parents think the content is innocent because the programming is geared for children, and in their day, a kid's show was a kid's show. It meant content geared for innocent children.

We were at the fair recently. A girl painted on the side of a disco ride had a low-cut shirt revealing implanted boobs, a 14-inch waist and 34-inch hips. I couldn't believe my eyes, that seductive pictures of women would boldly be displayed at a kid's amusement park. Isn't this supposed to be a safe place for children? Seeds of immorality are being planted everywhere.

What do the majority of parents think when confronted with these images? *Oh, well. It's OK,* and they continue to take their kids to these places without any explanation.

There are of two schools of thought I've noticed: shelter your kids, or let them see it all. As a parent, the choice is yours. But please make your decision and prepare your children based on wisdom and not laziness. Don't think, *Aw, what's it gonna hurt?* It will hurt; trust me. It will hurt you, it will hurt them, and it will make a difference—there's no question about it.

I don't believe in sheltering my kids.

Great! Then teach them what's right and wrong throughout the situation. Don't be at a carnival where soft pornography is being advertised to your children and ignore it. Sit them down and say, "You know what, son? That might look appealing to you, but let me tell you something. You will have a woman who will be honorable; she will honor her body and save herself for you alone."

Oh, let them see it all. They're gonna see it anyway. Let them figure it out on their own and maybe some day they'll work it out.

I'm sorry. Here's what I know. If you don't prepare them for the future somebody else will. There is a force preparing them for destruction, remember? If you don't intercede and combat this, they won't be able to stand. If you choose to let them see it all, then at least commit to grooming them to make the right decision every step of the way.

Many parents think, *Well, there's not much I can do about it anyway, so I'll not do anything at all.* That attitude is a road that leads straight to destruction and failure. If that's your attitude about child-rearing, then this attitude probably reflects your business ethics, too. A business owner with this attitude will cause his business to fail, and he will starve. It will cause problems in marriage, careers, and relationships, and it will definitely affect the children. They will never succeed in any endeavor, especially if they adopt this attitude.

Just because the problem is great does not give us the right to give in and give up. We are to set an example for our children. We set an example in the grocery store checkout line for our kids by turning around those magazines. We take a stand, which gives others the courage to do the same.

If you want your children (and your business) to prosper, then the attitude of least resistance has to be rejected. Decide right now if you will shelter or be lenient, allowing them to see it all. Either way, you should make up your mind *now!*

We've made the decision to raise our kids the same way we've raised companies, *by choosing the exposure that happens.* We shelter our kids by limiting their negative exposures and increasing positive exposures. This limits the opportunities for negative involvement and advancement and increases positive involvement and advancement.

I've been in marketing 20 years so I understand exposure. Pornography is just one example of the negative exposures affecting our kids. They are subjected to many other kinds of harmful influences. The media, for instance, leads our kids into believing it's all right to be broke and lazy. Even cartoons propagate this false concept.

In my many years of being in business, I understand that laziness equals poverty and that doing absolutely nothing is anything but "cool". In fact, on a biblical note God calls laziness wickedness. If you don't believe me, read Proverbs 6:9-11. A society that grooms and programs this lazy concept harms its population. Where is the future leadership for our country going to come from? Please help me. Tell me, where is it going to come from if all of our kids are being adversely programmed for immorality and indecency? Perversity is being programmed into them by outside influences—and this is happening right now. Kids are being programmed to be lazy and are hoping to win wealth. Nonsense!

I'm not saying to wage war against the media. You don't need to do that. But sitting around and doing nothing will not help either. Be a filter for your children regarding what they see and read. Media can be used to equip or destroy. Use it for equipping, but don't allow it to destroy your children's future.

In our *Creating a Dynasty* seminar, one of our exercises takes our clients back 30 years in television programming. We play old commercials they haven't seen or heard in years, and they can still finish the jingle. This amazes me that they can still remember programs they watched at age four or five. Some of our clients' memories stretch back even 40 to 50 years.

This confirms that children's minds can retain things for many years that they've been exposed to, and that those things are lodged within their subconscious minds. With that thought, realize that your children are daily being exposed to many harmful things. Besides exposure to pornography, mediocrity, and laziness, they are being exposed to idolatry in a huge way. Idolatry leads to greed and gluttony, which ultimately leads to destruction. Just look at our children today. This is the most obese generations ever raised because of their continual exposure to greed and gluttony.

Back to the process of *involvement;* a soft level of exposure initiates this process. Young people begin thinking, *Oh, that's kind of cool.* Then as they continue seeing multiple exposures over and over again, they enter the involvement process. This is when they start entertaining the idea or the subject matter and begin hearing, thinking, talking, and asking more about it. Their school friends are talking about *it.* Their teacher brings *it* up. Then another exposure happens at a friend's house while watching a movie together. At this point, they are clearly in the involvement phase when they begin openly expressing, "Wow! That's cool. I like that."

The best thing to do at any point is to analyze what your children are watching on television. Examine the cartoons that you allow them to see, and discern the messages being programmed into their minds. Look at how their belief system is being affected. Is it for real success or a fantasy of success? Look at game shows, like *The Millionaire* or *Wheel of Fortune.* What messages are they leading your children to believe? Does it make your children think that success is a mystery and happens to the "chosen few"?

Television, films, programs, you name it, are filled with fantasy. Success is not a mystery. It's about real, good old-fashioned hard work. That's why I believe in teaching kids how to work and work with excellence, how to learn new skills, get a job, or create their own business. Incidentally, so does the Bible. It contains many promises from God that they will receive if you will teach them the correct path, now.

> *Lazy hands make a man poor, but diligent hands bring wealth* (Proverbs 10:4).

> *All hard work brings a profit, but mere talk leads only to poverty* (Proverbs 14:23).

Do you see a man skilled in his work? He will serve before kings; he will not serve before obscure men (Proverbs 22:29).

He who works his land will have abundant food, but the one who chases fantasies will have his fill of poverty (Proverbs 28:19).

STEP 3—ADVANCE

When children reach this stage, they are fully addicted into pornography, which is idolatry. This is evident by their active search for more of *it*, regardless of what *it* is. It could be porn sites, a favorite show, an Internet game, or a current gadget fascination. If they talk compulsively about one particular character on television, which means that they are constantly thinking, dreaming, talking, and dressing like *it*, I'm sorry, but *it* is idolatry. Your concern should be to make sure that whoever the idol is, that *it* is worthy—and there is only one I know of who is worthy, and He is not an idol.

To sum up the process of ***Expose, Involve, and Advance:***

- *Expose* means to see or hear about something.

- *Involve* means to return for more.

- *Advance* means to be fully immersed with an intense craving for more. This is addiction (which is idolatry) because no matter what the cost, they want more and more and more.

ENDNOTES

1.   Michele Ybarra and Kimberly Mitchell, "Exposure to Internet Pornography among Children and Adolescents."

2.   www.safefamilies.org/sfStats.php.

3.   Estey & Bomberger, LLP, "Child Molestation & Sexual Abuse Statistics," www.childmolestationvictim.com/statistics.html (accessed July 3, 2009).

CHAPTER 4

PROTECTION VERSUS CONTROL

He who walks with the wise grows wise, but a companion of fools suffers harm.

—PROVERBS 13:20

Let's talk about the two concepts—protection and control. There is a huge difference between the two, and as a parent, you will need to decide which will be more beneficial in grooming your kids. You make the call; just make sure to communicate the difference between the two to your children.

PROTECTION

Protection sets your children up for success. It equips them to honor and to be honorable, and it provides rules that serve a consistent purpose. It sets up the parents as loving, thoughtful, and caring.

With this understanding in mind, if you really want to protect them, you'll explain why rules are in place and have to be followed. You'll explain that the rules are not about you becoming a dictator or commander—but helping them come up with solutions for their own protection.

When Arika was about 11, she asked me if she could go on a camping trip with one of her friends. I didn't see a problem with that because I knew the parents and thought the trip would be OK. So my answer was, "I'm pretty sure that will work out just fine. Go ahead and get yourself packed." (Well, I messed up and learned a big lesson from this.)

When we were getting ready to leave, Hans asked, "Where's she going?"

"She's going on a camping trip to the lake with Denise."

"Oh no she's not," he answered.

Arika was standing there, so I told her to allow us to talk privately. She went upstairs and then my husband explained, "Dani, I don't know what their standards are of protecting their daughter. How do I know that they're not going to let those two go on a bike ride up in the mountains by themselves? How do I know that they're going to keep an eye on them the way we would? Or that they will protect the way we protect—for their good, and not just to control? How do we know that?"

"I don't. I'm so sorry. Please, forgive me. I should have asked you first," I answered.

When Arika came downstairs, he sat down with her and explained, "Arika, God has appointed me to protect, guard, and govern you in love. My job is to make sure that I keep you safe and that I teach you how to keep yourself safe. I have to ultimately answer to God as to whether I've done a good job or not, and I don't know whether your friend's dad keeps the same standards that we do. I'm sure he does, but I can't take that chance because my job is to make sure to keep you safe."

Tears ran down her face, and she responded, "Thank you, Daddy, for protecting me." Her attitude was amazing. She unpacked her camping gear without complaining or murmuring because she under-stood that we loved her and were protecting her. She agreed to be safe and protected, so there was no rebellion. Amazing!

This situation could have been handled by Hans a totally dif-ferent way: "No! That's it and that's final. You're not going any-where!" That's lack of communication. This reveals a dictator and a control freak. To explain to your children that you're under a mandate from God to protect, guide, guard, and govern them is a much better way.

Arika, to this day, still has this amazing attitude when she's told she can't go a certain place. Her attitude is amazing because she knows that she knows that she knows—based on past communications with us—that our heart is for her to *succeed* and *excel*. Our hearts are set to see her *protected* and for her to be *wise*. She knows when we guide her that we have her best interests in mind, so she's able to accept yes or no from us.

Here's another way to offer protection to your children. About eight years ago, we moved my mom near us and successfully got her off of drugs. My daughter, Kristina, whom I had released for adop-tion, returned into our lives at the age of 14. When she turned 16 and began driving, she'd help my mom with grocery shopping and other errands. One particular day, a thought ran through my mind while I was visiting my mom, and I asked, "Mom, did you give Kristina the PIN number to your account?"

"Well, sure! She's my granddaughter. I trust her."

"Mom, I trust her, too," I said, "but here's what you need to under-stand. You can put an honest person in a situation without boundar-ies and turn that person into a dishonest one. I don't care how old that person is. This is tempting to anyone, especially a 16-year-old. It is better that you don't give her your PIN. Instead, set up a sepa-rate account with a separate PIN and deposit only what's needed and what's not tempting. Or simply write a check."

Here's the deal. An honest person lacking good boundaries or a good environment will be tempted to do dishonest things. The most dedicated husband, who is absolutely and passionately in love with his beautiful wife, can be placed on an island paradise with five or ten babes and be tempted. (I think there's a TV show about that.) I don't care how honorable a person he is. The bottom line is that we all buckle at one point or another.

I believe in protecting our kids and offering them the best percentage shot at success after I've equipped them to succeed. I wouldn't throw them out to the wolves just to see how they would perform. If I did, believe me, I'm sure I would see quite a performance. There's shock and then there's *real* shock.

CONTROL

Control is just the opposite of protection. Instead of setting up children for success, control sets them up for failure. It leads them to rebel and run. If you want to use this method to groom your kids, be a dictator and give them stupid rules that serve no purpose.

Control was used on me by the man who I thought was my father. He was a "control freak," an absolute *freak*. Breathing was even controlled by this man. I could never do anything or go anywhere, and no one was ever allowed to come to our house. He would make up rules and regulations out of thin air—all of a sudden, at that moment—and they wouldn't line up with the previous rules that he made or the last words that he spoke. This caused major resentment and bitterness because his rules were ever-changing, floating figments that were impossible to find or comprehend.

Protection was non-existent. In fact, he violated me, so that proved there was zero protection. It was all about control that accomplished only one thing—it caused me to run away at age 16.

Control dictates: "It's my way or the highway," which is a great way to get your children to rebel and hate your guts, just like I hated my dad.

Parents, I'm telling you, if you unreasonably constrain your kids, they will flee from you. If you try to control them, they will totally blow you off and say, "Forget it, man. You're a freak."

TRAINING YOUR KIDS

"Ever since the tele-seminar back in 2006, and since the release of the first edition of *Grooming the Next Generation* Home Study Course, not only has our whole family done a 180, there is peace and purpose in our home," writes Janina, one of our business clients. She says that their parenting and their children have dramatically improved, enhanced, and excelled in all areas.

"As the adults in the home, we were convicted to mature and lead ourselves and our children as God has intended. Now, with the second edition, it's taking us to even a whole new level." Recently they removed cable TV from their home and Janina's children, aged 7, 5, 5, and 3, request to watch our Grooming DVDs.

"People everywhere are always astounded at how happy and well-behaved our children are. What we have implanted into our children from this teaching has even our church members and church leaders talking and complimenting them and us. One pastor even called our children 'happily obedient.' There is so much more I can not even begin to start: unmerited favor, healings, baptism, professing Jesus to strangers, 1-2 grades above age level...Thank you. This is a life and a family I don't think I could have ever dreamed of but am so grateful for."

Train a child in the way he should go, and when he is old he will not turn from it (Proverbs 22:6).

God has qualified you to be a parent. He wants you to train up your children, and that it is a mandate.

Michael has six kids. Their ages are 7, 6, 4, 2, 1, and one due in February. "When we went for an ultrasound for our unborn baby, we were told that I would probably have to go out with the three younger kids who were with us." Afterward, the hospital staff commented that they hadn't had kids so well-behaved in a year.

"My wife says she's no longer *managing* the kids, now she's got freedom. I have a true alternative to angrily losing it with them. The future's bright with possibilities for us and our kids. Thank you!"

Several cultures around the world believe in grooming their children. I have a friend whose family line comes from India. His culture believes in grooming their kids to be highly educated, especially the ones who have passed through Europe and the United States. They're very respectful and responsible; they multitask and are multitalented.

This friend is a specialist of internal medicine who now owns his own hospital. He came to many of our training seminars years ago and says, "There is not a thing that I learned through those years of going through First Steps that I don't apply every single day."

His 15-year-old son was invited to Wimbledon for professional tennis. This teen had been groomed since he was young to have respect, honor, and self-discipline, but my friend wanted to hire me to help coach the mental part of his game. His physical skill level was amazing, but his mindset, confidence, and belief system needed further development.

I had an epiphany while standing there having this grooming discussion with my friend and began thinking, *Whoa! Why doesn't my culture do that?* In my personal experience, my parents had unintentionally (I'm sure) groomed me for failure, but what about other American children? Was this also happening to them? Talking to my friend reinforced my desire to teach this series to equip parents in successfully grooming their children.

The world is grooming our kids for something—you must understand this. The media, the government, and the public education system are grooming our kids for something, and this process is happening all the time. Outside influences from television, movies, music, video games, and the Internet constantly train our children. The attitudes, cultures, slogans, belief, habits, and views on authority, women, men, work, life, rights, and wrongs, are all coming through these avenues.

"Adults and teens [the average person] will spend nearly five months (3,518 hours) next year watching television, surfing the Internet, reading daily newspapers and listening to personal music devices, according to the 2007 U.S. Census Bureau's Statistical Abstract of the United States." Now, consider the process of exposure, involvement, and advancement and its effects on our children growing up and believing these influences.[1]

As a rule of thumb regarding DVDs or movies at the theater, before our kids can watch it, we have to see it first. Then, if it does not equip them positively nor align with our guidelines, they can't see it. Because I have seen the emotional impact the media has made on children, this rule is strictly enforced in our home. The media is so successful that children will remember commercial jingles or movie lines after one exposure. Even after watching it one time, they can regurgitate the lines flawlessly. That's why I want to make sure that the lines our kids regurgitate add to their success.

The media can be used to train your children to become fools or to be wise. You decide how it works. What goes in will come out—no question about it. So pay attention to the fruit that is going on in your family's life. Pay attention to what they're listening to and learning from and talking about because what they're being exposed to will absolutely come out of their mouths.

There are media tools that will help your kids dream and succeed, and there are others that will destroy their dreams and bring unnecessary complications to their lives. This I know: pornography, fantasies, and certain cartoons promoting laziness will complicate their lives. They won't understand why they're being lazy, but we know that they are being programmed by television to be that way.

> *He who walks with the wise grows wise, but a companion of fools suffers harm* (Proverbs 13:20).

To conclude, your children are constantly being trained and groomed. The question is, are you the one grooming and training them? Consider the answers to the following questions as you begin to examine the television programs and music they are watching and listening to, the games they are being allowed to play, and the Internet sites they are visiting. It's all about Expose, Involve, and Advance.

Are your children being groomed:

- To whine or win?

- To work with excellence or be welfare recipients?

- To have the reality of success or some stupid fantasy that will never happen?

- To have illicit sex, adultery, and/or pornography or to save themselves for marriage?

- To stand for something or violently fight for nothing?

- To be a moral human being or be involved with witchcraft and sorcery?

Even a child is known by his actions, by whether his conduct is pure and right (Proverbs 20:11).

God's promise to us is that if we will groom our children in His ways, when they are old they will not depart from them. There is a possibility that they may stray in the interim, but as they mature, they will return to their roots. This is a promise to you.

There are nine basic areas that I believe are important in *grooming the next generation*. I've listed these areas as strategies, and they will be the chapter headings for the remainder of this book. As parents, a game plan is needed to drive your children to success in all areas of their lives, for now and for their futures.

It's all about Expose, Involve, and Advance, and it's about programming your children for success.

If you have teens in your house, I promise you, it's not too late to start grooming them. I've seen thousands of our clients take this information to their teens and even have them go through the home study course. Afterward, these teens agree and take action, saying, "Mom and Dad, she's right. I want to do what's right. Yes, I have been tempted to do this and that." All kinds of confessions are made and the teens begin to transform into hard workers with a spirit of excellence from the exact opposite (lazy and apathetic). Thousands of these kinds of testimonials are archived in our database.

One of our clients reported that her 16-year-old would not get a job and constantly used them as an ATM machine. After listening to the audios in our home study coarse, the teen got a job on her own and a month later received a promotion to a management position. How crazy is that?

Parents, you would be amazed how much your children really want to please you. I know this to be true. Based on what I've seen in the marketplace, every teen and every adult wants to please their parents. Age doesn't matter.

As I've coached our clients on getting to the root of the hindrances preventing them from progressing to the next level of success, you'd be surprised how many times the parental-pleasing issue surfaces. Even a 65-year-old man with deceased parents said, "I've always tried to get the approval of my dad, and he never gave it to me."

"OK, well let's forgive him right now," I answered.

The desire for approval from our parents is something God placed in every kid. It begins with our earthly parents, and ultimately leads to seeking the approval of our heavenly Father. So regardless of whether you think it's a lost cause or not, *it isn't*. There is hope. I have many testimonies from our clients who thought it was too late and found out it wasn't. And it's not because I'm a great writer or teacher. It's because God's Word does not return void. That's why this will work. So either you believe His Word or you don't. This is where the rubber meets the road.

Regarding belief systems that need correcting, you may believe it's wrong to make money because of the culture in which you were raised. The ideals you were taught and the information you were exposed to created this belief system. This erroneous belief system has created a major problem for you in making money and seeing others make money. This extends also to those having a problem with the opposite sex. You were groomed to have faulty opinions and belief systems. Everything that we are today—who we are, what we believe, what we speak—is totally based on what we were groomed and trained to believe.

ENDNOTE

1.   Sami Beg, M.D., "Mass Media Exposure," www.abcnews.go.com/Health/story?id=2727587&page=1.

NINE
BASIC STRATEGIES

CHAPTER 5

STRATEGY #1: SPIRITUAL EQUIPPING

But if anyone causes one of these little ones who believe in me to sin, it would be better for him to have a large millstone hung around his neck and to be drowned in the depths of the sea.

—MATTHEW 18:6

OUR CHILDREN NEED TO BE SPIRITUALLY EQUIPPED

You may be wondering why this is the first strategy. I am shocked myself, especially because of my background with church and Christians. However, I must tell the truth of what has so massively equipped us for success. Please keep an open mind.

I truly believe that the Bible is the best success book that has ever been written. The principles in it have made me very wealthy and have helped me learn how to solve extremely complex issues that arise in all of our lives. In no way am I speaking from a religious platform.

If you have issues with religious people and what they have done with the Bible, I completely understand; however, I challenge you to read this very important section from a non-religious and an equipping for long-lasting success perspective.

We are raising a generation that is willing to stand for something great instead of falling for something stupid.

I remember our oldest son reading a book called *The Voice of the Martyrs* and the impact it had on him. He couldn't put it down. It's about men and women who died for a great cause, who were willing to take a risk, who stood for what they believed in, and who died for an upright cause. A significant part of his education involves reading the Bible and materials like that.

Recently, he asked me if I had the Bible on CD so it could play all night as he slept. I gave it to him, and now while he's sleeping, his spirit is being programmed with the goodness and purity of God's Word. Wisdom, financial help, success strategies for relationships, parenting, business and careers, as well as freedom for captives held in bondage are all contained in the Bible and are being deposited within him. So also is the ability to do what's right as a future father, husband, and businessman. His request for the Bible on CD fell right in line with the plans my husband and I had devised for him. This proved to us that our son was entirely in agreement with being groomed for success in every area of his life.

I believe these following points are absolutely necessary to groom children for spiritual success:

1. *Children need to be exposed to God.*

Imagine believing at an early age that God loves you, accepts you, and is proud of you just the way you are. What would that do to your confidence? Then imagine knowing that His love for you is so great that He grooms you into what He wants you to be because He has something perfect, something phenomenal, something greater in store for you. In order for you not to miss out on His blessings, He won't allow you to stay the same. Imagine growing up knowing this instead of the fear you may have been manipulated with and the blow you received from being hit over the head with the Bible. Imagine being taught to serve Him from a loving heart and the viewpoint of, "I don't want to do wrong because You love me so much, and I love You."

Imagine knowing as a child that God wants you to be successful in all areas of your life. How would this have affected you now as an adult? Imagine believing that He planted a dream within you that He will equip you to achieve. How would that knowledge have affected your life now?

I've worked with hundreds of thousands of adults and have done training seminars for years, but this one area really buckles people. Not believing that God approves of them, accepts them, or wants success for them is a common misconception for many people. But if they had been exposed to it as children, the growth and healing they must go through now would have been avoided.

2. Teach them that vision and purpose have been planted in them.

Our kids must know that God has a future, a hope, and plans of success for them (see Jer. 29:11). Equipped with that knowledge, they can be empowered to take risks, walk by faith, and declare this message of hope to others. Faith is enormous for every human being's chance for success. Lack of faith is one of the biggest causes of failure in adults. I'm not talking about religion; I'm talking about faith. Please don't get the two confused. They are very different. There are thousands who are not religious, but have faith in whatever they are doing, and they have experienced huge success. And on the other hand, I have come across countless religious people who have no faith in what they are doing and are consequently filled with worry, doubt, and hopelessness and have no vision. This kind of attitude cannot be passed down to our kids.

They need to know how God speaks, that He uses at least five methods to speak to them and is not limited to any one method. He speaks individually, through creation, through other people, and through circumstances—and all can be tested through His Word. All they have to do is pray, and according to John 15:7, answers will be given.

God really does speak to our children. So they should ask; He will hear and answer. *"My sheep listen to my voice..."* (John 10:27). A child has the capacity to hear His voice. The Scripture doesn't have a footnote that says sheep are only adults.

Our children have been taught to hear the voice of God through any means He desires to communicate and to seek His direction. We teach them to see situations that others would call "coincidences" as being confirmations from Heaven. For example, Roman asked for a guitar three years ago when he was 8. (He is the most persistent of all our children and the biggest salesman ever.)

"I want to play the guitar."

"That's awesome, Roman. Good for you, but Mommy is not buying a guitar!" He was very persistent with me, so I thought, *he's just picking an instrument because his older sister has a guitar and his older brother has drums.*

He was tireless in asking for a guitar. Over and over, it was "Mom, when can I get a guitar?"

Well, after much persistence, I finally said, "Here's the deal. I think you might want to ask your Father in Heaven because $200 is a lot to spend on a toy for an 8-year-old. So you might want to pray. If God really wants you to have a guitar, then you will have a guitar; either He will change my heart or a guitar will come from another place. You know Mommy hears from God, right?"

"Yes."

"If God tells me to buy you a guitar, then I will buy one. So stop asking me and start asking the One who is your Provider. I am not your provider, God is."

He prayed every night for a week until my friend, Paula, randomly called. I hadn't heard from her in months. She lives in the Bay Area, and we live in the mountains.

"Hey, I was cleaning out my garage and found two guitars that my sons totally lost interest in. Would your boys have any use for them?"

I almost dropped the phone. "Are you serious?"

"Yes. I'm going to be up there this weekend, and I'll just drop them off at your house."

Paula walked in with two electric guitars that were just what Roman wanted. He cried like a baby. It has been three years; he has not lost interest in his guitars, and I don't have to ride him to play them. He plays weekly and receives lessons at school, so no time is taken away from the house.

So that was definitely God. God built the faith of our son by answering his prayer, and faith is hugely important for success. This has been monumental because now he knows when he wants something to go to God, not just Mom and Dad. Now whenever he comes requesting something else, he knows the answer. At this time, he wants a snowboard, and I'm not buying a $500 snowboard for an 11-year-old. Can I afford it? Yes. Am I doing it? No. Sorry!

"I don't know why you're asking me. Why don't you pray and ask God? Your brother, Cabe, asked for the same thing when he was about your age, and he received the same answer. Why don't you pray and ask God? Someone gave Cabe the bindings, the board, the boots—everything, and that's the board Cabe is still using. So I don't know why you're asking me. You'd better start praying."

"OK...OK."

I reminded Roman of the guitars God gave him. "You prayed, you asked, and He gave. Not me; He did it!"

This builds their faith in Him, not in their parent's bank

account or in a Sugar Daddy. So keep reminding them again and again how God answers prayers. It's important; otherwise, what happens when Roman is 35 (and God forbid) he loses his job? Who should he trust as his Provider then? Do I want him to freak out and get on antidepressants because he can't provide for his family? Of course not.

So it's important for Roman, as well as our other children, to learn this lesson now. If they don't learn it now, it will be difficult to learn as an adult. At that point, they will have to unlearn all the wrong behaviors acquired as kids and then train themselves to step out in faith, trusting an invisible God to be their Provider. That's who I want them to go to for provision.

3. Teach them that through Him all things are possible!

How many times have you heard your kids say, "I can't!" or "I don't know how!" or "I can't do it!"? Many times, right? Well, they need to know that these statements are inaccurate and are excuses that limit their abilities.

Our children used to say this when they were young, so the first Scripture I taught them was Philippians 4:13, *"I can do all things through Christ who strengthens me"* (NKJV).

When they first say they can't do what I ask, instead of me debating, "Yes, you can. Get up there and do it," I'd say, "Hey, listen. Let me teach you something. Repeat this after me. 'Philippians 4:13—*I can do all things through Christ who strengthens me.'"* Here's Arika at two years old, barely able to speak, and certainly not clearly, but I'd have her to recite this Scripture. It didn't come out clearly, but she quoted it, just like all of our other children. These little kids could barely speak, but the voices of a victim and mediocrity tried to control their little tongues, even at those young, tender ages.

I had them repeat the verse twice, in order to help them memorize it. Here's why. The Word of God is far more powerful than my word or anybody else's, and it *will never return void.* God's Word accomplishes its intended purposes.

Whenever they say, "I can't!" I immediately say, "What's Philippians 4:13?" And they answer, *"I can do all things through Christ who strengthens me."*

"Now, go and do what you didn't think you could." Boom! They're off and running.

Now, I have a 16-year-old daughter who believes all things are possible for her. Talk about a risk-taker. Arika has written six songs. She earned her own money, went to Wisconsin and professionally recorded her music at the age of 15. Paying one-half of the production using her own funds (we were co-investors), Arika achieved the goal that she set a couple of years ago. Our risk-taker knows all things are possible for those who believe—and she believes. You can now find Arika's music on iTunes. This one has also traveled around the world caring for the poor.

Parents, don't train your kids to offer up excuses when you tell them to do something and they give an excuse why they didn't. An excuse is the voice of a victim and the voice of mediocrity trying to gain control over their tongues. As teenagers, they'll say, "I'm late from the party because…" some stupid, lame excuse we've trained them since age two to give us. That's right. Many of us teach our children that excuses are acceptable.

If we allow them to get away with "I can't" at two, we're training them to be victims and to be subjected to circumstances. We're training them that if they can give us a believable hard sell, we would buy anything from them.

To sum this up, anything our kids do, we've trained them to do. And as adults, if they haven't been taught differently, they will say, "I can't!" or use the excuse, "I was late because…"

How long will an employer or a client put up with excuses? The adults who can't keep a job or those who can't make a business work typically offer up ridiculous excuses instead of producing results. When an employer repeatedly hears, "I was late because..." their response is often, "Well, if that's your excuse, you're fired!"

4. Teach them the Word of God.

Paul, one of our clients, has had great success with our Grooming method. He and his wife started right away using the Word of God to groom their three girls in everyday life, teaching them first to memorize Philippians 4:13, like we did. "When our girls were learning to ride their bikes, they started to say they couldn't do it. We asked them what Philippians 4:13 said, and they would tell us; then we would tell them to go do it. They would go off and try again."

Show them how to lean on Him at an early age, and they will begin to see Him active in their everyday life. This is absolutely true.

Use the Bible to train for success as well as for correction.

- When they murmur and complain, teach them to *"do everything without complaining or arguing"* (Phil. 2:14). Our client Paul agrees. Referring to his children: "If they had a bad attitude, we would then ask them what Philippians 2:14 says, and they would say, *'Do all things without complaining or arguing.'* Then we ask them if they would like to try it again or should we discipline? Most of the time, their attitude changes. Overall, we are living from a different perspective, and people notice."

- When they have needs, teach them to *"ask, and it will be given to you; seek and you will find;*

knock and the door will be opened to you" (Matt. 7:7) I have countless stories that I could tell, just like Roman's guitar story. The point: I don't want them relying on man, but always to rely on God.

5. Teach them that they will go through trials.

Maturity will be produced in your children as a result of trials so that they lack nothing. Specifically, the things your children are struggling with, teach them to find the solution in the Bible. Plant this concept in them early so that they will be raised with this knowledge and will walk confidently in it.

> *Consider it pure joy, my brothers, whenever you face trials of many kinds, because you know that the testing of your faith develops perseverance. Perseverance must finish its work so that you may be mature and complete, not lacking anything* (James 1:2-4).

The phone call came in November 2008 in the middle of the night, the call that every parent dreads. Hans and I were on a weekend trip looking at some investments in Arkansas, and we had brought our youngest son, Micah, with us. One of my trusted girlfriends had the remaining tribe. The morning we left, Arika had a headache, and by the time we landed in Arkansas, she was throwing up. Our friend took her to the clinic where she received a shot to stop the vomiting. It worked for 12 hours; then in the middle of the night, it started back again.

At 4:22 A.M. Midwestern time, the caller informed us that Arika was in the emergency room at a local hospital and a CAT scan had just determined that her brain was bleeding. This precious angel of a child who had given us no trouble and had been compliant since Day One was suffering a double aneurysm with an AVM.[1] If there were wings assigned to a kid, this kid would get them hands down. She's been a dream child to raise and has set a great example in our community. She loves children and honors her parents, but now she was painfully suffering day and night.

Hans and I were frantic. We were in the Midwest and our plane wasn't scheduled to leave for another 24 hours. But God helped us all the way through this terrible ordeal and horrifying struggle. From having the pilot of a tiny plane speed up so we wouldn't miss our 20-minute California connection to miraculously saving our daughter's life, God was with us all.

Arika was rushed to Stanford University Hospital immediately after being diagnosed while Hans, Micah, and I were still more than halfway across the United States. It took at least three flights to get to our destination from a small town in Arkansas. We prayed the entire way. We asked God to allow us to make all of our connections and get us re-routed from Sacramento to San Francisco, which was closer to Stanford. Sure enough, God answered our prayers. Three seats were available without notice on three planes, and we made all of our connections!

By the time we got to the hospital and met with the brain surgeon and the neurologist, the double aneurysm and the AVM were confirmed. Arika suffered in ICU for seven days with vomiting and massive headaches because there was no way to alleviate the pain. She went through her first angiogram, CAT scan, MRI, beeping sounds 24/7, and strange people touching her body. She couldn't eat anything, and the medication she received for the pain made her vomit. In fact, everything was making her vomit, and she was losing weight like crazy.

I could not handle watching what I saw. As a mother, there is no hell like this hell. Remember, I was a kid who became a caregiver at the age of 11 for my mother, so I was familiar with hospitals and trauma and tragedies. But it didn't equip me for this phone call, nor did it equip me to watch our baby suffer like this.

Arika has stood for God since she was four and has always honored our family. She is reputable, gorgeous, and talented. She could be stuck-up, bratty, disrespectful, pig-headed, and stubborn. Instead, she was a dream child, a virgin, and only two months shy of her 17th birthday at that time. Home-schooled, Arika was scheduled to finish her junior and senior years early; and now, to sit and watch our dream child suffer?

It is one thing to watch your mother suffer as a child, but it's a completely different thing to watch your child suffering. There's nothing you can do. You're helpless. You're hopeless. The prognosis is not good; in fact, there's no good news.

I was sitting on the bed with Arika, trying to hold myself together, and she began to cry and ask the questions that run through everyone's mind when faced with a crisis: "Mom, why is this happening to me? I don't understand. Is there something that I've done? Is God mad at me?"

These questions came after days of vomiting and suffering massive headaches, after days of the doctors listing the options of radiology surgery or conventional surgery—opening her brain and cutting the AVM out. (It turns out that Arika was born with the AVM.)

When she asked me these questions, the answers had come only moments before. I was in the lobby with about 30 friends and extended family members who flew or drove in to be with Arika. (That's how well-loved this kid is.) Since only a few could be in her room at a time, I sat in the lobby. It was then I was reminded of a relative who also endured medical issues at 16 and how tragic it must have been for the parents, as well.

I flashed back to this person who fought cancer in her leg. She was a gorgeous, popular, talented athlete at the time. When I observed this relative going through her ordeal, I prayed, but I still had no clue what that family was experiencing. Trying to console and assist anyway I could still gave me no idea of the pain and mental agony they were suffering. Now I knew firsthand, and I had a whole new perspective and understanding of parents watching their children fighting for their lives. I've encountered many other parents going through similar ordeals—and I can now tell you through personal experience, it is hell. I've been to hell and back several times before in my life, suffering as a kid and as an adult, but there's nothing worse than watching your baby suffer.

Back in Arika's room before her scheduled procedure and before she asked me those questions, her doctors came in to prep us. They disclosed the facts and the risks of the surgery, such as stroke, blindness, and even death. (Arika already had suffered partial vision loss just from the bleeding.)

Then they added, "Arika, it's going to hurt because we'll have to keep you awake during the angiogram. Usually this procedure is done under sedation, but because the AVM is deeply inside your brain near your vision center, we'll have to keep you awake to prevent getting too close or touching it. "

"Can my Mom and Dad be in there with me?"

"No. You are going to be in there with a team of specialists." (The best brain surgeon in the world was on that team!)

As the doctors and my husband left the room, this is when Arika turned to me with her questions.

"Arika, those would also be my questions too because this has been really difficult to watch. But I know that God is faithful, and I believe that He is giving the Johnson family a chance to glorify Him. One of your cousins suffered with cancer in her leg at your same age. You were very young at the time, so you don't remember—not only did she survive, she is now a married woman and has a very successful career in the medical field.

"Our trials are to produce perseverance and to make us mature, lacking in nothing. You're the same age as she was, and she was also in her junior year. She was beautiful, popular, loved—all of that. And people were asking the same questions, 'Why her?'

"So I have something for you to think about. You wrote a song called 'Another Day' and you said in that song that you would worship Him when trials come as though it's your last day. So, girl, God inspired you to write that song, and it prepared you for this day. You have never been through anything as horrible as this, now you can relate to people who have suffered intense horrible circumstances. Either we're going to be a Christian family that worships Him in the good *and* bad times or we will reject Him as soon as trials come and times get hard. Here is your Another Day."

She began to cry and said, "No, I will not be that kind of Christian. I will worship Him through whatever it is that happens to me. I will be one who stands for Him in good times and in bad." And her eyes began to sparkle, which was the first time I saw that in five days. In that sparkle she saw the purpose for her affliction. "I will worship Him regardless of the circumstance."

"This is going to humble adults and children," I said, "and you'll be with your friends again. This time when you hear them talking about something pointless, like high school gossip and who's dating who, you'll look at them and say, 'You've got to be kidding me! You're worried about something like this? There are so many things that matter far more than that.'"

Arika started to smile, and I continued. "Once you make a stand for Christ, this story will inspire adults to get over themselves and their little problems. This story of how you loved Him through this affliction will be told, and He will get the glory for pulling you out of it, versus others whose affliction counts for nothing. But with this affliction, Arika, you are going to come out stronger in your faith and lead many to Christ. So, Arika, you have nothing to worry about. God is faithful to His word, and He will help you through this. He promises a long life for those who honor their parents, and you have clearly honored your father and me. You're gonna make it girl, and thousands are gonna hear about it."

Right after my talk with Arika, the doctors performed the surgery and were able to treat 90 percent of the AVM, which was far more than they thought they would be able to reach. This also meant that there was a small chance another bleed could happen due to the remaining 10 percent AVM.

After a couple of days of observation in ICU, Arika was sent home in a wheelchair, unable to use her legs due to nerve damage. She was underweight, but the vomiting had stopped. To make matters worse, *Creating a Dynasty*, our advanced training seminar that occurs twice a year, was scheduled for the following weekend, and I had little time to prepare. Eight hundred people were registered to arrive in Atlanta from all over the world, so making that meeting was a real concern for us. We asked the doctors the soonest Arika could fly since there was no way I could leave her. I was shocked when the doctors said she was fine to fly at any time.

Arika arrived home five days before we needed to leave for *Dynasty*, but her condition was not improving. It was Friday night, and all she wanted to do was watch movies and eat her favorite meals, so I cooked all of her favorite meals and desserts. *It's time to fatten the kid up because she's lost so much weight.*

When Monday came, Arika was at home, the boys at school, Hans was at the office, and I was in bed crying. I was emotionally, physically, mentally, and spiritually drained. I wanted to cancel the event and stay home with my baby who had been through so much yet was blessed to be alive. I also knew what it took to conduct *Dynasty* spiritually, physically, emotionally, and mentally. I would be standing and speaking for three days and nights, for hours and hours.

The week prior to this tragedy, I discovered that all of the *Dynasty* exercises and training materials were gone, nowhere to be found. They were possibly stolen by my former assistant, which meant that I would have to rewrite the entire three-day and night seminar. That fact alone was enough to send me over the edge. Rescheduling the event was very tempting, even though clients worldwide planned to be in attendance.

There is no way I can do this, I thought. I would have to rewrite the materials, pack, and then somehow use the remaining days to recover from this horrific, nasty trial that was an absolute living hell.

While Arika was in the hospital, I was found in a corner crying and shaking for a couple of hours. I had simply lost it. Three times I shut down and no one could bring me back. It was total overload for me, totally.

Isn't that enough to put somebody in the mental hospital? The seminar materials were missing. Our daughter couldn't walk, and we had just suffered through an amazing trauma.

I began to waver. *I think we can cancel! Our clients love our family and believe what we teach. They know that family comes first, and they know that's the way we live. We teach them also how to live keeping family first. If we have to pay for some of their plane tickets—$2,000 to $5,000 apiece—so be it. They'll understand.*

At this time, Arika couldn't bathe, soak, dress, or do anything for herself. So I placed her in the bathtub to soak. It was Tuesday—*if we're going to Dynasty, we'll have to leave the next day.*

"Arika, I think we're going to cancel *Dynasty* and stay home."

"No, you can't do that, Mom!" Fire was in her eyes.

"Arika, listen. Our clients love us, and we love them; and they'll understand because we live what we teach. You're a higher priority over *Dynasty*. That's my work, but you're a higher priority."

"Mom, you can't cancel. I don't care if I go in a wheelchair; that doesn't matter to me. I want to go!"

"Arika, I don't want you to think it's your fault and that's why you don't want me to cancel. I've been speaking for 18 years and have never cancelled an event. I've nursed all of you guys on breaks, and I've never cancelled an event, not once. I didn't even cancel the event that was scheduled one week after I gave birth to Cabe. With my back issues, I've never cancelled, and that's a pretty good track record. This would be the first time I've cancelled in all the years I've spoken at events. It's OK to cancel one; that will still be an amazing track record. I have no problem canceling, and it will be a good example for our clients."

Again she said, "No."

"Why don't you want me to cancel?"

"I want to go!"

"Why do you want to go?"

"Mom, those people are flying from all over the world because they want change. They desire change. I want to be with this rare breed of people…people who desire change for their lives. That's who I want to be around this weekend. I don't want to be here, and I don't care if I have to be in a wheelchair all the way there and back. It doesn't matter to me. You can't cancel that event." Arika then asked me a very probing question, "So, why do you want to cancel it?"

What do I say to that?

"Arika, I know you know that my last assistant may have stolen all of my materials, and I am not ready."

"Well, that sounds like an excuse, Mom, and you taught me that excuses are not allowed. We are not canceling this event, Mom. I want to go, and that's where I want to be." That's when she started crying, and this blew my mind.

"There is nothing that makes me happier than watching my mom being used by God to change people's lives," she continued. "There is nothing more that I want to see, right now than seeing the hopeless get hope. There is nothing I want to see more than God using my mom. We are going to be in Atlanta this weekend, and God is going to change their lives."

I went from the absolute lowest I've ever been in my life—headaches, body aches, no energy—to, "All right, let's do this thing."

I texted Jenn who is our event director, Arika's former nanny 17 years ago, and my very close friend. She had watched Arika grow up and wouldn't leave her bedside during this trauma; she had stayed and suffered the entire week at the hospital with us. I knew that I would need Jenn's energy to put this event on.

My text said, "The event is on, and reschedule the two TV interviews as well. We're going after all of it!" (I had previously cancelled these events due to Arika's condition, but now everything had a green light.)

As we pushed Arika in a wheelchair through the airport, she was smiling at people every step of the way, even though she had a headache that the doctors said could last months. There was no shame, only confidence that her God would take care of her legs. Arika was going, not for a miracle for herself, but to see miracles happen for others; she was in a wheelchair smiling the whole weekend.

My instructions to her and the staff were to answer any questions about why she was in a wheelchair this way: "Wait until Sunday, and then we'll let you know." (It would only be natural for people to ask since she attended every event, singing on stage.)

Friday night, separate from our business and leadership seminar, we had the opportunity to pray for our clients in a very personal way (all 800 of them). So, I'm praying for people, and I call Arika up and prayed over the swelling in her brain and the brain damage that she had received. She returned to her wheelchair, still not walking; then I requested she sing, 'Another Day.' She sang until after midnight; we continued praying for everyone. On Sunday, Arika woke up healed and walking. She showered and dressed herself, walked down to the conference room, and worked that entire day. That night, as we ended the seminar, I told the whole story and people wept as they heard it.

"Don't ever underestimate the Spirit of inspiration that comes from Heaven because just three days ago, I was going to cancel this event. There was nothing in me that could do it. Yes, your fearless leader who has been speaking boldly all weekend—let me tell you what our family went through just a week-and-a-half, ago. Arika! Step forward!"

She came forward, wiggling her legs, dancing, and stomping on the stage because God had completely healed the nerve damage, and He received a standing ovation.

Immediately after we returned home, letters and emails came flooding in. One woman, who walked in shame and guilt after her daughter suffered from an aneurysm years ago, wrote a testimonial. She thought that God had forsaken them during their trial, so she left Him also and went the metaphysical route.

"I now walk with Jesus because of the testimony I heard Sunday night. Now I know that God was not mad at me or my daughter and that this trial was meant to persevere and mature us. It was to build our faith, and my faith has been built. Here I thought that these three days were the most life-changing event I'd ever experienced in my life, but the last 20 minutes overshadowed this powerful event. The last 20 minutes of hearing that story saved my life. I went home to my daughter who is now 9 years old and told her Arika's story. I finished saying, 'You will stand for God with this affliction, and you will say how God has healed you because He has.'"

> *In this you greatly rejoice, though now for a little while you may have had to suffer grief in all kinds of trials. These have come so that your faith—of greater worth than gold, which perishes even though refined by fire—may be proved genuine and may result in praise, glory and honor when Jesus Christ is revealed* (1 Peter 1:6-7).

6. *Teach them to serve others.*

Today we live in a generation of spoiled-rotten kids who think only of themselves. It's a "give me now" generation. But you *don't* have to raise a spoiled-rotten brat; you can turn this situation into something good.

Here's the outrageous truth. We sent Arika at age 11 to a phenomenal outreach in San Francisco that does amazing things with youth, teaching them how to serve in the trenches. As the youngest member of the team, Arika lived on the streets with the homeless from a camouflaged bus. She served them, washed their feet, cut their hair, and made sandwiches for them. This little, wealthy kid from Northern California scrubbed the feet of the homeless in San Francisco as well as picked up trash and other debris.

This experience totally ruined her. It ruined her to the point that a month later, while at a five-star restaurant in San Francisco, she looked out the windows and down on the streets, and said, "Mommy, there's one of my homeys."

My mother and my oldest daughter were with us enjoying an extravagant meal when she said this. Then she quickly added, "I'm sorry, but if it's OK with you, I want to give my food to the homeless."

We each packaged up our food into five separate containers and went walking through the streets of San Francisco with my daughter. My little girl would find someone and say, "God wanted me to tell you that He loves you. Is there anything I can pray for you about?"

One man said, "Yes. I have gangrene in my feet. I think they'll have to be amputated."

Arika and I got on our knees, put our hands on this man's feet, and she began to weep while praying for him.

So let me say this again. You don't have to raise spoiled brats. Our children have been very blessed financially, but we refuse to spoil them. As mentioned previously, once in a great while they'll say "so-and-so has a Nintendo," or "so-and-so has an Xbox," or "so-and-so just got an iPod or iPhone." Our response is: "Good for them! But just because those things are available doesn't mean it's wise to buy them."

So this is the deal. You don't want spoiled-rotten brats who say, "Give me...give me...give me.... I want...I want...I want.... I need this outfit. I've got to shop over there. I've got to make sure I have the most 'in' clothes." Instead, help your children become well-rounded with a good perspective on life.

My kids and I wear clothes from Wal-Mart and hand-me-downs from each other and from friends, and I'm a multimillionaire. I let them see real life by taking them beyond the border—that's reality. To a certain extent, what's in America *just ain't real.*

For years our family has helped others through what we call "Secret Blessings." Every Christmas, instead of doing the traditional celebration, we teach our children to become well-rounded by giving to others in our community. Our friends know not to buy our children anything because they don't need anything. They've got everything they need. But families in our community, on the other hand, are in real need; so that's who we bless. We suggest that the amount they would have spent on our family be pooled with ours and secretly used as a blessing for someone else.

After finding a needy family, we personalize our gift shopping just for them. Our kids spend the money shopping so that way they're involved in the entire process. They shop for the food, clothing, and other gifts we give; and the response is phenomenal.

"I'm going to give this to Joey," they may shout. They've never met Joey and may never meet Joey, but we show up at Joey's house with a truckload of gifts, a month's worth of food, blankets, clothing, and jackets. Our kids buy items that they may have wanted for themselves and then totally give it all away.

Let me tell you what this experience does for them. Once while vacationing in Hawaii, we did Secret Blessings to the local Hawaiians. On our way home, I asked our children what was their favorite activity on the trip and they unanimously answered, "Giving gifts to the poor and giving to the homeless kids."

Can you imagine? Giving was what they loved the most. It wasn't the beach or boogie-boarding. It wasn't the restaurants or other fun activities. It wasn't the trip, at all. It was what happened in their hearts when they gave from their hearts. They've learned this valuable lesson at very young ages.

Cabe's fifth year birthday party was huge. I mean, he was lavished with a ridiculous amount of gifts. When everybody left, we sat him down and said, "Cabe, you know what? There's a little boy who's having his birthday today, but there's no party for him. His mom and dad can't afford it because they're living in a shelter, right now. Cabe, would you like to bless a little boy who does not have this kind of blessing?"

"Yes! Where is he?" he asked.

"Pick five things that you want to keep," I answered, "and we'll put the rest in the car and deliver it right now."

And that's just what we did. Our 5-year-old son denied himself in order to give to somebody in need. This is the heart that he's been trained and groomed to have. It is an unselfish heart that's eager to give. Our son is not different from any other boy. All kids have selfish tendencies that can be groomed to help them in future dealings as spouses, parents, and career or business people.

7. They need to know that God is not boring and that He is active.

He's alive. He's here. He's now. If you're in a boring church, then your kids are probably also bored, and what young person wants a boring relationship with anyone, especially an invisible God? If this continues, their relationship with Him has a great chance of also being boring, and it could possibly be maintained from a distance. Your child may be physically present, but mentally they're somewhere else. This is what happens when something doesn't appeal to them. They shut it out.

The world is offering our children fun, wildness, and crazy activities. Some of them are living on the edge and being exposed to excitement and wild energy outside of the walls of the church. This is what your children want to experience. They are a generation who wants to see signs and wonders. You should let them see wild and crazy things in their spiritual experience, too.

For example, Acquire the Fire is a group who has put together events where 10,000 young people come together for concerts, day-and-night all over the country. That's wild! That's fun! The difference with this concert in comparison with worldly ones is that the guy on the stage is not being idolized or lifted up. This is peer pressure at its best—youth encouraging each other to do what's good, holy, and right rather than being pressured to sneak out and have sex.

There are various youth conferences available that we send our kids to. These conferences have great music and relevant speakers who are stylish, fun, and have something worth saying. Some have awesome testimonies of being druggies who've since come to Christ in a radical way. Our kids have seen radical moves of God because a radical generation absolutely wants to see that.

We've sent Arika and Cabe and their youth group to these conferences several times so that they could experience being around a bunch of risk-takers who are excited about God. These kids pray for the sick and travel the world helping those in need. They have a fervent fire to do something great, and we want our kids to be around those who are like-minded.

None of these organizations are perfect, but the fruit that results from them is amazing versus the alternatives, which are other influential people they could be hanging out with or looking up to. Now, they are looking up to a bunch of people who have turned their lives around and are not ashamed to say where they came from and what their past was and how God changed their lives. These guys look the way this generation wants to look; they are not a bunch of boring-looking people. They are a people who can relate to the generation that's on the earth right now.

One organization pulled one million kids together to fast and pray. Another campaign brought 400,000 kids to Washington, DC, for 12 hours of fasting and praying. I've been to one of these events with 75,000 youth crying out to God. Some of them are pierced, tattooed, and dressed like a lot of kids today, but without revealing cleavage and skulls tattooed on them. They have radical music and amazing testimonies. (I'd much rather see them crying out to God and being peer-pressured in that manner than being pressured to go against God and righteousness.)

This *next generation* is a retaliatory, picketing generation, just like in the '60s. Since this is the flavor of this generation, you'd better have them retaliating for what is right, rather than what's evil. That's what these organizations are doing. They are stirring the youth to righteousness. They stand at the Supreme Court quietly protesting abortion with red stickers on their mouth that proclaim, "Life." This is better for them, to stand for their beliefs that abortion is wrong and abstinence is right.

This is the wild, risky, and fun stuff your children want. So allow them to be exposed to it. Allow them to meet a God who is alive, who cares about them, and who's doing wild things in the marketplace. Don't just allow them to be shut up in some boring situation. I'm telling you that they want the *wild*. God put the *wild* in them, so allow them be exposed to it. You'll be amazed at what will happen in them as a result.

We've groomed several of our kids by placing them in a wild environment, and now no one can stop them from believing that they will succeed or that the sky is the limit. They know that God is real, alive, and involved in their daily lives.

8. Teach them to pray.

Teach them to seek Him first and to talk to Him. Teach them how to pray, and then pray with them. Encourage them to cry out to their Maker, and as a result, their faith will grow in leaps and bounds.

Give them opportunities to lead family prayer. Our kids are the ones who lead prayer at our house. "OK, whose turn is it—yours? OK, you pray."

Our kids have been raised in an environment of prayer. When they were really young (2, 3, and 5) and fell and scratched their knees, I would do this cute little thing that I believe started them on a foundation of leaning on God and prayer. Instead of seeking consolation from man, they would seek it from God.

When they fell or hurt themselves in any manner and would come screaming to me, I would say, "Self-control" and they would stop crying immediately. (Self-control is a fruit of the Spirit and it is the Word of God, which *will not return void*.)

"Show me where it hurts." They'd show me, and then I'd ask them if they wanted Jesus to take the pain away. They'd either say yes or nod their heads yes. Then I would put their little hand on the spot with mine on top and ask them to repeat the prayer after me. In this manner, they would learn how to pray and ask God to heal them.

"Jesus, please take the pain away, in Jesus' name, amen." Then I would grab the pain off of their knee (or wherever it was) and ask them where they wanted me to throw it.

"Throw it on the ground or throw it over there!"

I'd throw it wherever they said to throw it, and they would run off to play. What normally could have been a big hysterical scene that some kids use to manipulate is now reduced to nothing.

Do you know that some people are taught to be hypochondriacs through the attention they get by hurting themselves? By using this alternative method, we distract them by using the Word of God to teach them how to pray. God takes the pain away and gets all the glory, and we get instant results.

This method is truly foundational also because it causes them to turn to the Lord in their own personal time of need. Our kids pray for other kids, each other, and themselves. It was awesome seeing that fruit in them when they were so little.

"Mom, I want to play drums," says Cabe around his 12th birthday.

"Wow, that's awesome. Good for you."

He kept asking, finally suggesting we buy him one for his birthday.

"That's a pretty big present for a 12th birthday," I said. Drum sets are about $500. Our stance on this is that we're not going to make an investment in something that they may lose interest in. He became pretty persistent until I told him, "You need to ask your God because right now I don't feel it in me to pay out $500 for a drum set. So, your God will have to be the one to change my heart or somehow provide a drum set for you. I don't know if someone will give you an old drum set to practice on or not."

He started praying, "God, change Mom's heart."

God was the One who woke up this drummer instinct in him, but I didn't know that at the time. For all I knew, this kid would use the drum set for a year and then lose interest in it. Then we would have a drum set that we would need to get rid of. So I'm looking for the parent who bought a drum set and their child lost interest in it, so we can take it off there hands at a reduced price. There is always someone looking to give away their kid's stuff that they lost interest in, just like my friend Paula and the guitars.

I just kept telling Cabe, "You need to pray. You need to pray."

Two days before his birthday, after dropping the kids off at school, I was on my way back home and I was playing a CD in my car.

The song started off quietly with cymbals, and just then while driving my car, a scene popped into my mind. I believe it was a vision from God. There was our son, Cabe, as a young man on a stage with really long hair, and a microphone attached to some big headphones. His hands were beating the drums and playing the song that I was listening to on my CD player. He was really going for it and sweating. Then suddenly, there was a large band with backup vocals. Then the scene pans out, and I see a huge sea of people who are all totally into what was being played.

I began to weep and say, "OK, God. I got it. I got it."

So God changed my heart, and He was the One to tell me to buy the drum set. That day I went back to the house and my father-in-law happened to come down for the big party weekend for the three birthdays—Cabe's, my husband's, and my father-in-law's. I asked him, "Can you help me? The Lord just told me to buy a drum set."

I had to go immediately because this was not what I had planned for his birthday present. So we went shopping, my father-in-law set up the drums, and locked them in the barn.

The night of the party was so precious. Everyone was praying for the birthday guys when Cabe suddenly burst out with, "God, please change Mom's heart about drums. I really want a drum set." We all said "Amen" and began eating. After the other presents were opened, Kristina announced that she needed to go buy formula for our grand-baby and wanted Cabe to go with her. He reluctantly agreed.

As they left, I quickly moved everybody (about 50 or more people) to the barn where the drum set was hidden. In the meantime, Kristina texted me that she was returning with the excuse that she left her wallet in the barn and needed Cabe to retrieve it. Cabe thought everybody was still in the main house when he opened the door to the barn and flicked on the light. Everyone was silent; then his eyes fell on the drum set. We all screamed "Surprise!" He ran to me bawling for a few minutes, just absolutely sobbing and holding me tightly. "Oh Mom! Thank you, God! Thank you!"

"Come on; let's see what you can do," I said.

He sat down and started playing. He was amazing, phenomenal, a natural drummer with perfect timing. Our son got to see that God is above his parents, so if God placed something in him, God had the power to change his parents' heart. I was dead set against it, no way were we buying drums. Cabe understood this, but would not let it go because God placed the desire in him. This confirmed Cabe's heart to play the drums, so it was powerful for Cabe to see that his God was his Provider. When I told him about the vision, he wept some more.

Today, Cabe plays the drums daily and the barn is now a music studio full of instruments. Arika plays the guitar and piano. She started playing the piano when she was about six. Cabe has the drums, Roman the guitars, and Micah plays piano as well.

So our kids know how to pray for what they want or to pray if they're having nightmares.

This is the culture in which our children are being raised.

9. Look for the fruit of idolatry.

> *Even while these people were worshiping the Lord they were serving their idols. To this day their children and grandchildren continue to do as their fathers did* (2 Kings 17:41).

This is alarming. In other words, it's like saying, "You know, while you're worshiping the Lord at church, you're serving your idols at home." This is sobering.

Idolatry is the practice of worshiping an idol, which can be a person, place, or thing. It is the thing that reigns supreme in one's life other than God. It's giving the position or prominence to anything above Him. If a person's thoughts constantly revolve around one thing, well, that's idolatry. This is so hugely important to understand because we have become an idolatrous nation. I believe we live in idolatry, and it is accepted more now than at any other time in our history. Ours is a nation full of idolatry, and here's why. (Most people don't even realize this because our idolatry is so sneaky.)

In our country, we don't idolize graven images, per se. The majority of us aren't bowing down to wooden structures, golden calves, or statues representing an idol that's been formed by hand or tool. But I will tell you this, we live in a culture so deceptive that celebrities, movie stars, and singers are idolized. Basketball and football players are idolized. Characters in movies, such as Darth Vader, Anakin Skywalker, etc., are idolized. Possessions, houses, boats, and cars are idolized. (Oh, I guess they are wooden or metal images formed by man's hand, now aren't they?)

We have parents who are trying to keep up with the neighbors, so day care centers have been raising the past few generations. Why? For what? A Lexus, an exotic vacation, a bigger house, expensive furniture—all of those things are idols. We're sacrificing our kids in order to keep the possessions that we think we must have in order to be accepted in our society. People are sacrificing their children for more money, higher positions, and better reputations.

That's exactly what happened in the Bible days. Read through the Books of Ezekiel and Jeremiah. The people in those days sacrificed their babies at the altar of Baal because Baal was a fertility god and it was believed that Baal had the power to prosper their land, their sheep, and their women. It was all about money, and it is all about money today, too.

Money, fear, and addiction reign in many lives. Whatever the internal driving force in operation, or the thing talked about the most, that's what's being idolized. I believe from personal experience (that I don't have time to write about now) that if God isn't first, your spouse second, children third, and your work last, then it is quite possible that you have a problem with idolatry.

Idolatry was one of the major things I struggled with early in my career. Several times greed got the best of me. And according to the

Bible, greed is idolatry. *"Put to death, therefore, whatever belongs to your earthly nature: sexual immorality, impurity, lust, evil desires and greed, which is idolatry"* (Colossians 3:5).

When I was an aspiring new business person, I idolized millionaires and everything they said. They were as gods to me, and everything they said was law. Then when I gave my life to the Lord, I idolized pastors and evangelists. I studied and studied what they had to say, never even thinking that I should read the Bible myself, cover-to-cover.

Since then, I've learned that no man behind any pulpit or in any business should be idolized. Their words will be tested by the fire and in many cases will probably not survive. Only the Word of the Living God will survive.

Historically, idolatry is the breaking point where God says, "That's it! I'm wiping them out!" And He does. Mercy goes out the door. He will put up with adultery, murder, lying, cheating, and stealing for hundreds of years, but boy, when you start worshiping other gods— now, you're in big trouble.

So in our children, I look for the *fruit* of idolatry. If they are going to succeed, they can't do it with idolatry in their life. It will destroy them. I have personally watched marriages, families, health, and finances destroyed because of idolatry. It's so sneaky most people don't notice it so they're unaware that they are walking in it.

At one time, a lazy, stinking cartoon character that I can't stand somehow slipped into our house in the form of a present for one of our children. It was a movie of this particular cartoon character, and it soon became the center of attention in our home.

I heard our boys quoting pathetic lines from this character. Stupid lines like: "It's fun to be lazy. Oh, it's so awesome; we don't have to do nothing." After they began regurgitating those lines, suddenly every conversation was about "so-and-so..." (That character again, and again, and again.)

After hearing about this character for the umpteenth time, I finally spoke up one night while we all sat at the dinner table. "You know guys? Mommy's job is to groom you for success. Do you want to succeed, or do you want to fail?"

"We want to succeed," they all chimed.

"Do you want to be powerful and influential men who make a difference in people's lives and are loved by many, or do you want to be someone who affects no one and does nothing with life?"

"We want to be successful, loved by lots of people."

"Great! Well, let me tell you something. What you're showing me is that somebody else has taken the place of your God because all I hear you talk about, all I see you play, and all I've seen you watch is this one character. This thing has slipped in and has taken the place of your God, so I want you to make a decision right now. For one week, I don't want you to watch it, talk about it, relive scenes, play with it, or even mention its name."

They looked at me and said, "OK, Mommy."

"You need to ask God to forgive you for the sin of idolatry because idolatry will lead you to the pit of hell. It will destroy everything in your life. It leads people to divorce court since their priorities are out of whack. It leads parents to desert their children because of addiction to drugs, alcohol, pornography, and material stuff. Addictions are idols. You can be addicted to success, which is also idolatry. So if idolatry is what's happening here, we need to make sure that your hearts are clean and that you do the right thing now."

Our boys made the choice right then and there, and for the next seven days they didn't talk about it, watch it, play it, or relive it. They held each other accountable. Whenever one of them even accidentally began to mention it, they'd catch themselves and say, "Oops," bite their tongue, and change the subject.

Fear of failure, fear of success, fear of rejection, fear of people, etc., is another form of idolatry. Fear constantly occupies the minds and wills of many.

"I'm afraid."

"I can't leave my house because I'm afraid."

"I can't pick up the phone because I'm afraid."

Many are bowing down to the idol of fear. Fear of man, which is being fearful of people's opinions of you, is the reason why some won't step up and do what needs to be done. Teach your kids that fearing what others think leads them to mediocrity and failure—never to success. What God thinks of us is far more important.

The fear of man causes one to think, *Oh, what will people think of me? What will they say?*

Some of you are probably worried about what I wrote earlier regarding the media. "My kids are going to hate me when I tell them they can't watch that particular show or that I will cancel cable altogether." But they won't hate you if you explain the difference between protection and control, between failure and success, between 98 and 2 percent. Then ask them what they want to do in the future. "What's your hope? What's your dream?" Allow them to make a conscious choice because in their hearts they already know the right and wrong thing to do.

Friend, I've watched idolatry rob people blind. I've watched it ruin people's lives. It slips in simply and then steals everything of value, including lives. I've witnessed it robbing me. I lived the life of idolatry, and I nearly lost everything because of it. It ruined my life for a while, and now I will do whatever it takes to protect my children from falling into that same trap—no question about it.

Money is a great tool, but when you love it and chase it more than anything else, it becomes your god. The *love* of money, not money itself, is idolatry. At one time, that idol ruled my life. Everything was second to it, and I thought I was a "Christian." How about that?

10. Teach your kids how to read the Bible.

There is never an age too early for your children to read straight out of the Bible. I've had ours start as early as the first grade. This is how they discover who God is. I have various kids at different places in the Bible now because of different rates of speed and different ages.

Cabe started reading the Bible many years ago. He came home in the first grade and said he wanted to read the Book of Job. He was an avid reader even in the first grade. And he understood what he was reading. So we taught them to read the Bible starting from Genesis to Revelation and to ask God to instruct and give revelation. I want our kids to know Him and to understand that He is an awesome God.

Do you want to know when I started to understand the Bible? It was through reading the Toddler's Bible to my babies at night. That's when the hunger to read it began surging in me. The stories were very simple and basic, but they caused me to cry when I would get deep revelation about who He is and what He has done for His people. This gave me a hunger to be used by Him and a want to learn His voice, His character, and His ways.

Then the Lord began revealing to me issues about our nation and its direction. This is when I found out about the destruction that is coming on this land. It was through reading the Bible that He began to show this to me—judgments because of idolatry and abortion. As I was reading through the Bible, I realized that we are just like the people that He would discipline with a painful judgment, because He disciplines those He loves and it hurts Him to see us destroying ourselves.

I began to see God the way He really is and that it wasn't about people being perfect in man's idea of perfection. No. God didn't choose or work with perfect people. He works with imperfect people, people who screwed up, lied, and stole. He's a redeeming God, and you wouldn't know that unless you read the entire Bible.

What provokes His blessings? What provokes His wrath? You can learn some from a Sunday morning message, but it's just not enough. You can learn some from a Bible study or through some other man's book; however, it is still not enough, and you risk being misled to believing things about God that are simply not true. Most people have hundreds of books written by men and women that they've read from the Foreword to the Epilogue. But the Bible is the only book that is not read from cover-to-cover, start to finish. People read it in sections starting with their favorite.

The Bible tells us that it is an abomination to depend on others for understanding. We are supposed to lean on Him. I want our kids to depend on our God and not on man. I want them to dwell among man and be an influence to man, but I want them to be influenced by God and His Word, which is the Bible. Unfortunately today, some people in the pulpit have never read the Bible cover-to-cover. Most ministers speak solely from their own Christian experience and from their own mental strongholds, doctrines, and theological twists. If they haven't read it cover-to-cover, they don't know Him or His character or what provokes His blessings or His judgment.

Pastors have personally confessed to me that in seminary they weren't required to read the entire Bible. In fact, they only read commentaries written by man. Bible school students have confessed the same thing. As students of a pastoral degree in a four-year college, they were never required to read the Bible cover-to-cover. Instead, they read man's commentaries on their perceptions of the Bible. This is dangerous and unbelievably scary.

The Bible is not boring. It contains a lot of meat. Contained within is wisdom about how to succeed in all areas of life; marriage, parenting, problem-solving. It offers strategies on how to triumph in regard to relationships, faith, struggles, and trials. So much wisdom and advice is contained throughout the entire Word of God that it's amazing that we're so quick to ask a friend for advice instead of asking

God. In the Old Testament, you'll also discover God's character and reasons for the instructions He gave.

I've wept through the Bible, and I've received awesome revelations from it, as well as conviction, wisdom, and knowledge. This is information I want our children to have access to, plus I want them to lean on Him themselves.

So, let's sum this up. *Spiritual Equipping* is the first area of grooming for your kids. This is accomplished by taking the following steps:

1. Exposing them to God. They must realize that God loves them, accepts them, wants them to succeed, and is preparing something great for them. God has planted something in each child.

2. Teach them that through God all things are possible. Remember, when "I can't" comes up, teach them the Word, and then with God's help, have them do what they thought they couldn't do.

3. Teach them the Word because it doesn't return void. Don't just teach them baby stories; put the real Word of God into them.

4. Teach them that they will go through trials.

5. Teach them how to serve others as well as to feed the homeless or give Secret Blessings. Make it a new family tradition for the holidays.

6. Teach them that God is not boring.

7. Teach them how to pray.

8. Protect them from idolatry by looking for the *fruit* of it in their lives and help protect them from that trap.

9. Teach your children to read the Bible cover-to-cover. It will really make a difference in their relationship with God and help them to gain wisdom, knowledge, and understanding.

Each one of these areas, if lacking in you as the parent, needs to be established and settled in you. Learn together. Don't allow another day to pass without being spiritually equipped and helping your children to be spiritually equipped.

ENDNOTE

1. AVM: Arteriovenous Malformations, masses of abnormal blood vessels in the brain.

CHAPTER 6

STRATEGY #2: SELF-IMAGE

For as he thinketh in his heart, so is he.
—Proverbs 23:7 (KJV)

TEACH YOUR CHILDREN TO HAVE A HEALTHY SELF-IMAGE!

In our coaching, the topic of *self-image* is one of the top five challenges that many adults struggle with. I've witnessed that it is one of the greatest deterrents in an adult's life, whether a multimillionaire executive or a stay-at-home mother. Many people from every sector across the board are afflicted with low self-esteem, and its effect on them is deadly.

My personal self-image was not groomed very well, so I identify with these people. In fact, my self-image was absolutely awful. I was told that I was fat, ugly, and stupid and couldn't do anything right. This assessment was made by a stepfather (the man who raised me) who was strung out on drugs at every possible moment. I watched my parents do drugs and abuse their bodies my entire childhood; and as a result, every insecurity issue imaginable belonged to me. I struggled with rejection and abandonment issues, especially after finding out that my dad wasn't my biological father.

I was a little girl who wouldn't wear a bathing suit around my friends or play with them dressed in a bathing suit because of an unhealthy self-image. I was very uncomfortable when it came to my body. (I've learned that this is what happens when you see your father looking lustfully at you or molesting you or when wicked curse words are spoken over your life.)

In actuality, as a teen, I was in great shape with a flat "6-pack" stomach and ripped arms and thighs. I was a competitive athlete who could "hoop it up" and go head-to-head with any guy. I was the kind of girl who would give them a good run for their money, if not beat the "snot" out of them, embarrassing them to pieces.

I was in great shape (as most of us were when we were young), but I had a fear of being heavy. This fear came as a result of growing up with a 280-pound mother who chose to abuse her body; a father who weighed 350 pounds; and two sisters who topped out at 300 pounds each. This fear was so intense that I became anorexic at 18 after my father and boyfriend convinced me that I was fat—when, of course, I wasn't.

> *Death and life are in the power of the tongue* (Proverbs 18:21 KJV).

Because I heard the words "you're fat...you're fat...you're fat... you're ugly...you're stupid...you can't do anything right," ringing in my ears for years, it formed my self-image. I adopted these words as the truth. It took years before that lie was discovered and broken off of me because it was also wrapped with pride.

Pride is an unhealthy self-image; it's seeking the approval of man—something I continued to do for years.

Am I now trying to win the approval of men, or of God? Or am I trying to please men? If I were still trying to please men, I would not be a servant of Christ (Galatians 1:10).

From age 18 to 22, I gained and lost 50 pounds four times in four years. I starved myself. I had been on one-half tuna sandwiches a day and still gained 35 pounds in a month. Why? An unhealthy self-image will do that to you. *Your children's self-image largely comes from **you!***

Let me explain. Women, if your daughter sees you taking hours to get dressed and hears you constantly making negative comments about your weight or appearance, she will adopt an unhealthy self-image and an unrealistic model to live up to. If you daily spend too many hours exercising, overly vain in your pursuit of perfection, then she may choose to follow your example.

Some women eat fat-free this and fat-free that and spend too much time on themselves. Then on the other hand, there are those who let themselves go and should probably reverse that trend. Their little girl is watching and probably saying, "I don't want to be like her."

That was me. My mom and sisters were severely overweight, so my objective was to be nothing like them. On certain holidays my mom would spruce herself up a little, but she was a drug addict, so she looked like what she was every other day of the year.

Mothers, your little girls are watching you and some are already caught at one extreme or the other. The Barbie-doll image is the self-image constantly being projected at them. So whatever you do in excess, will absolutely negatively impact them.

If you've rejected your body and self-image, your daughters are possibly rejecting theirs, too. That is a weakness rooted in fear; and fearful people are easily controlled. They're completely ruled by today's society, which is all about fitting in and looking good. All of that self-image nonsense will eventually drown an individual.

I had to go through a lot of inner healing and forgiveness because of the bad self-image placed on me by my parents. So make sure that you're grooming your young daughters and sons to have a healthy self-image in Christ. Make sure that they are not churchy or religious about it, just wise.

I've coached thousands and thousands of clients of all ages, from teens to those in their 80s, and I will tell you that they all have something in common—a self-image problem that prevents them from taking risks, talking to certain types of people, or trusting anybody. This is huge! Problems of this sort are groomed into kids by their family first and then their peers.

Because we see adults suffering from self-image problems every day, this was the area we chose to address initially with our children. We didn't want our daughters unrealistically striving to have perfect bodies or their lives so wrapped up in what their butts looked like in a pair of jeans. We wanted their image to be healthy and unique, the way God designed them, because the way He formed them takes His breath away. He loves how He fashioned them and the way they look (their noses, eyes, hair, etc.).

I know that God placed within every single human being the desire to please Him. This desire to please our Father in Heaven may be deeply embedded within us, but it is placed there in order for us to eventually search Him out.

Our mistake is trying to please man instead of God.

BODY IMAGE

If you've noticed that your children are not comfortable in their skin, fix it. Address pride because pride seeks the approval of others; it tries to appeal to others rather than embracing its own uniqueness. This happens as they move into adolescence, although it frequently may appear long before that stage, and sometimes as early as ages 4-6.

Some kids are very conscious of their bodies at a very young age. Just watch the young girls dance and see who they are trying to please or whose attention they are trying to attract. Little boys want to look cool by wearing the right sweatshirt, pants, and shoes. This may occur very early, even long before adolescence. Usually, adolescence is the stage when you begin to see the fruit of your training during the very early stages, that is, what you did or didn't do. This is also the time when peer pressure is at its highest.

So pay attention to the signs of their embarrassment toward their bodies because this shows an issue of the heart. Discern and then sit down with them and have a heart-to-heart talk. Find out the motivation for "why" there's an issue with their body and why the discomfort. Search this out because even from a young age, this translates into unhealthy actions for any adult.

After living with several teenagers, I've noticed that they get a little weird about their bodies at this season in their lives. To counteract this, I talk them through it. It's a must. I start off by saying that I also felt the same way at their age.

BE WISE AND IMMUNIZE

When I say "immunize," I'm not talking about inoculations. I'm talking about preparing your children for the often rebellious stage that they will be encountering. When our kids near those often rebellious teen years, I confront them head-on by putting these questions out in the open so there is awareness of their actions and of the traps set for them.

- "Are you going to be one of those teenagers who hates their parents?"

- "Are you still going to love me when you are 13?"

- "Are you still going to sit on Mommy's lap when you're 14 and 15?"

- "Are you still going to honor me when you're that age? A lot of 13-year-old kids hate their parents and talk behind their parents' backs."

I begin disarming and immunizing them at the ages of 9 through 11 by planting these seeds. At these ages they are so sweet, and if you're consistent in training them right, not too much will change as far as their obedience, cooperation, and training goes. It's when they shift into the teen gear that something happens within them and life may become a bit chaotic. They begin spreading their wings, testing their boundaries and their strength.

God knows that this happens, and to be honest with you, we've messed with the biblical clock. In biblical days, girls married between the ages of 12 and 14 because their sexual nature awakened at that time, making them ready for marriage. Boys were called "men" at that age. Were they fully developed? No, but their bodies were ready for marriage.

Our modern lifestyle doesn't fit the biblical timetable for our teens to marry at puberty. If our teens aren't groomed correctly to wait until their 20s for marriage, they will have problems holding out.

So this is what we do with our teens. We tell them when they hit 12 that they are on their own in regard to their relationship with God.

"You're not under our covering any longer. It's up to you to find God and make amends with Him for yourself. We've led you to Christ, but now it's up to you to live out what you have learned."

I immunize them, something we do in the business world as well. I do this with our clients. I do this when training sales forces and staff members.

"Listen, here's where we're heading. Hard times are coming and this is the way we're going to combat them." That's immunizing people.

Immunizing your child begins when they're still kissing you 15 times a day before they reach their teens.

"Are you going to be this way when you're 13, or will you be like most teens who hate their moms and gossip at school behind their backs?"

"No, Mom. I'll never be like that."

They all answer like this, but this gives me a platform when rebellion begins to rise up to say, "Hey, remember when we had that talk? I asked you if you were going to be like those teens who hate their mother."

Challenges like this we've not experienced with Arika. She has been an amazing child and the easiest in the world to raise. But when Cabe turned 13, he took a *stupid pill* for a moment. Now he's back to being our son again. No joke! All of a sudden he forgot how to act and that we were the parents and he was the son. As he was approaching that rebellious age, I asked him, "Are you are going to be one of those teenagers who hates their parents?"

"No, I don't want to be one of them," he quickly answered.

"Awesome! So if I see you going in that direction, do I have permission to say something to help you to succeed so that you're not one of them?"

"Yes, please."

So, when he swallowed that stupid pill, I addressed the issue. "Cabe, do you remember when Mommy had that talk with you about being one of those teenagers who hates their parents?"

"Yes!"

"And remember you gave me permission to say something if I saw you going in that direction?"

"Yes."

"And you know it's because I love you?"

"Yes."

"You're in one of those moments!"

"Oh, I'm sorry, Mom. Please, forgive me."

That's how it goes. Just that simple and he's back to being "normal" Cabe again, an amazing son with an amazing future of leadership. Oh and by the way, he is now 15, a big, athletic, gorgeous young man who still sits on my lap and kisses and hugs me throughout the day. Arika is almost 18, two inches taller than me, and still does the same: hugs and kisses and sits on my lap everyday. I am truly blessed. So be wise and immunize.

CLOTHING

Boys and girls are prone to "becoming" whatever they choose to wear. If your child is "all caught up" in a certain style of clothing and is completely fanatical about it, then there needs to be a talk about pride. Being fanatical about a particular style of clothing means they need to wear it in order to feel good. For instance, in the case of a particular brand of jeans, I inform them that the jeans are not the issue; the jeans only show the "fruit" of what's in their heart. (They need to be aware of this, as well as you.)

Where do kids get this stuff? Mainly from watching you, as well as from outside forces. If you live in greed, they live in greed, and you've set them up for poverty. If your kids *must* have the best name-brands, ask yourself why. If they're all wrapped up in their clothes in order to feel good, then they are set up for absolute failure. If they must wear the "in" thing and be part of the "in" crowd, there's a huge problem brewing. It shows that their identity is being established in an image that will burn out and conforms to the 98 percent rule, which leads to mediocrity.

Instead, set their identity in the uniqueness of their form. Teach them not to care what other people think. Let them know about the great prize they possess in being set apart and made different for a unique purpose. God did the same with Esther; her unique purpose was to lead the children of Israel at a crucial time in their history. God uses different people with different looks for different times. Check out John the Baptist. He was totally and uniquely different. Although his father was the high priest and wore all the priestly garments and followed all the traditions of the religious, John the Baptist did not. People of that time would have thought that to have been very rebellious. He would be judged in our time as a hippy or a tree hugger, yet God used him to prepare the way for the Lord.

Often times many in the Church curse beauty, but beauty is Scriptural. Look at Sarah and Rebecca. They were so beautiful that kings wanted them as their wives and their husbands lied, saying they were sisters because they feared losing their lives. Beauty is not frowned upon in the Bible, but it is in some Christian circles. If Esther wasn't beautiful, she would not have been chosen as a candidate, through a beauty contest, to be queen, and she wouldn't have been in a position to save her people.

I don't want to say that our daughters should not strive to be beautiful because that's wrong, too. I'm saying, whether our daughters are beautiful or not, they will grow up knowing that they are and that their beauty is not only set on outward appearances but on who they are on the inside as well. They will be taught to embrace the uniqueness of their form and character.

I've watched Cabe go through this season with "skinny jeans"; so don't think that your sons are immune to this type of issue regarding clothing. Guys are absolutely subject to it and infected by it. This is where pride sneaks in.

Cabe wanted to wear skinny jeans so badly that it prompted me to have some hard talks with him about his self-image.

"But, Mom, I've got to wear these jeans. They've got to be washed so I can wear them."

"Really? Interesting! So what? You don't feel cool in baggy jeans?"

"No. I just don't like them."

"Really? So you don't feel good if you're not wearing those skinny jeans?"

He's wiggling in his little skinny jeans as we were talking.

Here's our rule concerning out-of-control thinking:

"Cabe, in order to make sure that skinny jeans haven't become too high of a priority in your life, let's give them a rest for a couple of days. This is just to make sure that your heart isn't set too high on them, so we're going to say 'no' to the skinny jeans just for two days."

Guess what I see in his heart now? I see a change. I see the idolatry of those skinny jeans being defeated, and I see his heart of pride humbled as he says, "OK, Mom, I agree with you. I don't want anything to control me or defeat me."

Why? Cabe has to win; that's what his personality is about. (We'll talk later about different personalities.) When Cabe sees something else trying to win over him, he'll quickly go in the opposite direction.

Our son is way too cute for his own good. Cabe has the full package. He's hotter than hot. He's a drummer, he's an amazing star athlete, he's smart, and he's the teacher's pet. So guess what I have to groom into him? Humility! I have to groom humility in him to know that his favor comes from God. His favor as a drummer and an athlete, his education, his favor with teachers and human-kind all come from God. It doesn't come because Cabe is great; it is because God gave him great natural ability in these areas. Favor doesn't come because Cabe is a great athlete. God is the One who made him a great athlete. Now Cabe's part is to give God his best by working with a spirit of excellence and staying humble by giving

God the credit for his success. This is the point we have to make sure he understands.

So this is how we've groomed him: "Cabe, this favor is not for your name to be made great, but for you to follow God. Your looks, talents, and abilities are to be pointed in one direction, and that's toward the One who gave it to you. God has a plan for this influence in your life. As you are recognized for your abilities, you are to glorify your God and tell others about Him who has blessed you."

The world, ego, and pride would love to sift our boy like wheat, so he has to be groomed to succeed. We don't want him walking onto the court knowing he's the star player. Instead, we want him to humble himself before his coach with this attitude: "I'll do anything you tell me to do." We want him to honor his coach with his eyes and respond, "Yes, sir."

Cabe's humility had to be groomed within him in order to combat his natural personality of being self-reliant and over-confident. He's the big "honcho" on the block and the most popular boy in school. Cabe loves seeing miracles. He prays and listens to the Bible all night long and is a worshiper on the drums. Because of this, we realize that ego and pride will tempt him for the next four years as well as the rest of his life, so it's mandatory for us to continue to groom him for long term success by teaching him humility.

Teach your children to accept themselves and embrace the uniqueness of who they are. With that accomplished, a unique identity that's completely their own will emerge. Caution them to prevent their identity from ever being rooted into someone else's identity, hairstyle, conduct, or style of talking. It is a must that your child is raised to be their own unique self.

Many people comment about each of our kids' uniqueness and differences. This is by design, not by default. We've taught our kids to embrace their own unique assets and liabilities. Worrying about fitting in with others or what other people think is something I groom them not to do. As stated before, this is the fear of man and will prove to be a snare.

When children don't learn these lessons, they will walk in the fear of rejection. They'll take offense resulting in the "fruit" of their identity becoming unstable and insecure. People with the fear of rejection always think others are out to get them and no one is for them. This line of character and immaturity needs to be erased and groomed out of them. It's self-sabotage and a major issue that I've seen in tens of thousands of adults.

Most adults are motivated by fear, so they do things that hold them back without realizing it. This leads to self-destruction and causes them to become self-absorbed. Keeping your kids out of this pattern now will help them from becoming wounded adults. If left unheeded, your children will not take risks, and they will end up like most people, full of excuses and living a mediocre life at best.

BOUNDARIES

Arika has gotten a lot of attention from boys since she was 4. When she turned 16, she was allowed to date with our blessings and guidelines. We had an approved dating list—but for about six months, no one asked. Boys wanted to date her, but were afraid to ask. That's perfect because the rule is they have to ask her father, and her father wants to work out with them first. That's just to make sure that the date can protect her. (Yeah, right.) It really was a self-weeding process.

Hans is a kickboxer, though, so a work out with him is kickboxing. ("Whoops, that was a little too hard. Let me help you up," says Hans to a potential suitor.) They take one look at him and say, "No way."

By the way, the date is supervised with Mom, Dad, or brothers. Why? Because I know this about people from years of working with them; you can put the most honest, pure person in a situation that will cause them to fail. No human being can withstand total temptation without God's help. And all it takes is one second for you to give in, and it's "game over."

We discussed this earlier in regard to protection and control. We believe in helping our kids to succeed by protecting them and not controlling them. One is a dictatorship; the other is a mutual agreement between both parties with the same goal in mind. (If you haven't had this conversation with your children yet, don't hesitate—do it now.)

Our job with Arika is to help her succeed with her goal. If it means supervised dates, then that's just what it will be. Not because she's not trustworthy, but because she is! Because she has an honorable goal, we're going to help her succeed in that goal. Arika doesn't walk away from this rule thinking that we don't trust her; instead, she thanks us for the protection, again and again.

Any woman or man left to themselves will lead themselves into destruction.

I believe this. Look at David, the apple of God's eye. He had it all—money, wives, children, wealth, fame, and everyone's love. But in one moment without accountability, he fell with Bathsheba into sexual sin. His men were off to war, and he should have been right there with them. Instead, he was left wide open with zero accountability. The result was sexual sin and murder when he shed the innocent blood of Bathsheba's husband. The apple of God's eye—a warrior, a worshiper, a king over Israel, and chosen by God—had everything. David was a man after God's heart with pure worship, a good guy, an awesome character, but when left with no accountability and placed in a situation where he couldn't say no, he fell.

So what makes you think that your kids won't fall? What makes you think that they will grow up in this world stronger than King David? Your expectations are too high. Don't put them in situations where they are going to fall. If you do, then you are setting them up for failure. Many have set their kids up for failure due to the absence of boundaries. Our children don't go to sleepovers unless I know the standards of the parents. Will they go to bed and leave the girls unattended? Will their friend's boyfriend sneak into the house at night? These are things I don't know and quite honestly, things I don't want to know. So to keep it simple, there are no sleepovers.

Do our kids have a life? Yes. Our kids have a great life and they enjoy it. Our kids are not deprived, and they are happy. They don't know what they're missing, and to be honest with you, they're not missing anything, anyway! Think about it. What exactly are they missing from a sleepover?

1. Getting no sleep.

2. Laughing about something stupid.

3. Gossiping about their friends and others.

4. Being pressured to do something they don't want to do.

5. Being allowed the opportunity to do something that they may regret for the rest of their lives.

Is that what they're missing? Also, by the way, they rarely go to other people's homes. They can have friends to our house, but rarely are they allowed to hang out at other people's houses. The only exceptions are those whom we strongly approve of and raise their kids the same way we do. And that's very, very few. Why? I'm setting our kids up to succeed and not to fail. It's all about protection. If I don't know who the husband or wife is, I don't know what kind of evil they may speak over our kids. But friends who raise their kids like we do are trusted with our kids. (This amounts to less than five families.)

What does that mean? Simply this: I make sure that Hans and I are the ones grooming our kids. Our kids are thankful and don't feel controlled or squelched. They feel protected, and when a child feels protected, they feel loved.

BOUNDARIES FOR DATING

We use a simple strategy to establish dating boundaries. This process has proven beneficial for Arika and all concerned because it sets everyone up for success in this area. When she and the young man go through this process, they both emerge understanding the concept of Arika's value to us and God; and she understands her own self-worth and value and has a healthy self-image of honor and respect. It's a win-win situation for everyone,

In our strategy, there are three stages to the dating relationship and at least three other issues of great importance to us. Basically, these stages outline our plan for them to begin a casual relationship that gradually progresses and builds as they decide to proceed to the next level. (This also depends on our assessment of their ability to remain trustworthy.)

We've set a foundation for Arika even before we arrived at this dating age, and we continue to stress these points to her. It's real simple! If any young man doesn't come through the head of the household, then that relationship is not honored by God. If the young man makes an appointment to meet with us, then he is going through the proper channel. But anyone (including our children) who tries to go behind our backs will have a dishonorable relationship that won't go well with them. It could possibly lead to pregnancy or other disasters.

It is mandatory that the young man interested in Arika make an appointment with Hans and me. We all sit at the kitchen table and have a non-threatening conversation that is meant to disarm, open communications, and begin establishing a relationship between all parties.

The first thing we do is to open the conversation with prayer and then participate in the following line of communication. Everyone is given the opportunity to verbalize their expectations in the dating process and everything is laid out on the kitchen table. The following is a sample of our initial conversation that begins with us really building up the young man.

Stage 1—Getting to Know Each Other

"Meeting with us says a lot about your character and courage. It shows that you actually have the right intentions and the right training by your parents, who've established this honor and courage in you. Because you and Arika have proven yourselves honorable, we want to respect your position of honor by setting up some healthy boundaries for the two of you to succeed in. Thank you for your honor."

Next, we explain that the two of them are someone else's spouse and that God will use their relationship as a training ground for future relationships.

"Arika is someone's future wife and you're someone's future husband. How would you want to honor somebody else's future spouse? The way that God works is, if we can be trusted with this relationship and learn to honor, communicate, and value safe boundaries with each other, then God will trust you with a bigger responsibility for the next relationship, which could possibly be with your future spouse. So this relationship is actually a training ground for marriage someday. Whether you're chosen for each other is not known right now. But we do know that God will use this opportunity to train you to become a future spouse. So how you communicate, respect, and honor each other, how you learn to iron out differences and embrace each other's assets and liabilities—things of that nature—are training tools for what's to come."

Stage 2—Trial Period

At this point, we talk about our expectations for the dating part of their relationship.

"There will be a trial period which takes place at our home. You're welcome at our home to hang out, have dinner, and spend time on the weekends when we do family activities. This way you'll get to know us and we'll get to know you and see how you two are interacting.

"Always make sure that others are around in whatever room you are in. Obviously, Arika's room, or any room behind closed doors, is not acceptable because this will put you in a compromising position, which we know that you don't want to be in. Because we trust and honor what you are exemplifying as a young man of good character, we want to uphold that honor for you and Arika as well, especially since Arika is a young woman of good character and honor. Again, it's not because we don't trust you; it's because we want to help you succeed."

Stage 3—Supervised Dates

We drop this bombshell next.

We actually have Arika share her goal of being a virgin on her wedding night and her plan for achieving that goal is no time alone with the opposite sex. We then say to the young man, "As you just heard from her mouth, Arika's goal is to remain a virgin on her wedding night, and she has agreed to healthy boundaries in order to achieve this. I'm sure that you'll honor that, as well. So, supervised dates at all times with other people is what we suggest. These people can be Hans and me, or it could be one of her brothers tagging along on a date. That way, you'll always be in a position to remain honorable with accountability. So we're going to set you and Arika up to succeed."

Stage 4—Double Dates with Other Couples

This is the final stage in our dating plan.

"After we go through a series of supervised dating and you've proven yourselves strong, capable, and totally honorable, then we can move to the next stage, which is double dating with other couples. This stage includes dates with Hans and me, but also allows you the option of dating with other couples who share similar goals and whom we are confident have good boundaries and uphold them."

Other Guidelines

At this point, we establish other guidelines that will govern their relationship. This process is meant to weed out any riff-raff or less than honorable guy who doesn't value a virgin. (This doesn't mean that she hasn't been pursued by some of those types, but because he has to sit through this conversation and abide by our standards, it says a lot about him, especially if he still wants to date her afterward.) Arika, on the other hand, feels like a chosen princess who is valued by her parents because of this process. She sits there smiling the every step of the way.

- **Phone Calls, E-mails, and Facebook** (or any Internet social network)

  "We are a family that truly believes in keeping God first. But this is what typically happens when we become fond of somebody else—it becomes really easy to remove God from first place. So in order to keep Him in first place, we have healthy boundaries when it comes to the phone, as well as other forms of communication. Arika has a 15-minute quota on the phone, so she will not be staying up all night talking. Regarding e-mail, which we don't do a lot of, be aware that it may be checked. Keep this question uppermost in your mind: do I want Arika's parents to read what I just wrote? And Arika, would you want us, or anybody else for that matter, to read what you just wrote?

"If something happens that's not honorable, it will eventually be revealed to us. We will find out about it. Arika can tell you from personal experience this does happen. Again, the whole thing is to keep the relationship moving in a good and positive direction, and we are all for it."

- **The Heart Issue**

"We have groomed Arika to guard her heart, and we suggest you do this, too. Always keep God in the first position. If He is in first position, then accountability will also be there.

"At this time, you are truly being trained to succeed in a future, lifelong relationship with somebody because this area truly needs training. It does not come naturally or easy for anybody. Keeping God first in this dating situation is the most important thing for Arika and us."

- **Touching**

Then we talk about having a plan for "touch." We talk about the possibilities of temptation in the future and how to combat it, especially if the relationship progresses into exclusivity. Then we drop the next "bombshell." We ask the young man again another pointed, hard question that he was not expecting. "So what is your physical plan?" They usually say, "What do you mean? I don't understand what you're asking?" "Arika's goal is to remain a virgin so how will you help her achieve that goal? When we say 'physical plan,' we are talking about boundaries for touch and everything else that comes with it."

We suggest *Passport to Purity*, even though Arika has already completed this series. We don't know if he has, but we believe that it's important for him to do so, too. Then we suggest that they study it together at our kitchen table.

"This whole thing is to take pressure off of you so that you both know what to expect in this relationship. *Passport to Purity* consists of audios and a workbook of different scenarios that a couple can get themselves into. You're going to have to make decisions beforehand not to get into those kinds of situations."

This next part we address with a smile on our faces.

"There does come a point where the brain shuts off and says, 'No' and the body takes over saying, 'Yes.' We want to help you two succeed and not end up in that kind of temptation where you are compromising your goals and your personal dreams. It's very easy for this to happen. So Arika, what's your plan?"

"I'm not kissing until my wedding night."

"Great! Now, how does that work for you, young man? I trust that you are an honorable young man and you'll honor her decision to save her mouth for her wedding day. So that means staying away from anything that would lead to that. Her mouth is set apart for somebody else.

If that person is you, then it will be yours at that time."

- **Influence**

  Parents, as this relationship progresses, be aware of the comments your teen makes in passing regarding the person they're dating. For example, you might hear something like this:

  "Mike doesn't want me to cut my hair; he likes it long."

  "He wants me to wear a dress, instead."

  "He doesn't want me to go to that college."

  If your teen begins to indicate through certain comments that the person he or she is dating has too much influence over them too quickly, then it's time to have the "98/2" conversation with them. It's time to remind them of their identity and that this is part of learning how to be in a relationship.

  "Quickly handing over your identity to another human being that you're simply dating and getting to know is very dangerous for your future. In this relationship, it's important for you to be who God has designed you to be, how He formed you, and how He delights in you. Don't change your image and who God has trained you up to be just to gain approval or recognition from another human being."

  Gently remind them of what you taught them during grade school when they were trying to please others by conforming to a certain way of look, talk, style, or dress in order to gain recognition. Make sure this is a loving conversation. Then tell them that this is another testing point.

"This is very dangerous as a child, very dangerous in a dating relationship, and even more dangerous in a marriage. 'Am I going to change all that God has made me to be to make this one person happy?'"

At times, I go on to add how I almost ended my life because of Brent's disapproval of my looks, size, dress. When he finally broke up with me, calling me all of the horrible names that he used to say throughout our relationship, I felt worthless, useless, and unlovable. Why? Because I tried to be everything that he would have loved me to be, but no matter what I changed, it was never ever good enough.

Be consistent in hearing what your teen is saying. Look for the level of influence that this person and relationship has on their life. Make sure that they are holding strong and not conforming to what somebody else wants them to be.

- **Questions and Answers**
  We open the floor for questions, and then answer each one.

- **Conclusion**
  After we address all of their questions, we conclude with these statements:
  "We trust you, and we appreciate you for

coming. This says a lot about your courage and your character. If you ever have a question or need help with the relationship, feel free to call us at any time. If you need ideas about activities, feel free to ask. If you feel like you're ready to go on a double date with someone else, ask us. We will use your conduct and how trustworthy you've been with this part of the relationship to determine our comfort level and whether we agree that Arika's ready."

Then we close in prayer, asking God for His protection, guidance, and wisdom over them.

It's all about setting them up for success rather than putting them in a compromising position to fail. Here's what's so beautiful about this: Arika has been treated like a princess and a prize to be won. She has been totally honored; doors are opened for her and chairs are pulled out at lunch. The fact that they have to endure this process shows Arika's value to us, to God, and to herself. Then, quite naturally, there is an expectation on everyone's part to uphold that value.

It has been amazingly successful, and Arika has held others accountable in this way as well. She gladly tells her friends what her standards are and suggests that they live by the same standards. These standards have not scared guys away from asking; however, they have kept our daughter safe and maintained a healthy self-image of honor and respect.

CHAPTER 7

STRATEGY #3: PEOPLE SKILLS

YOUR CHILDREN DESPERATELY
NEED PEOPLE SKILLS!

People skills are mandatory if you want to see your children succeed now and in the future, but sadly, they are sorely missing in today's society. A generation of parents and children who know nothing about honor and respect is the result—that's why we'll address this skill first.

In marriages, parenting, businesses, churches, and so forth, we've noticed the lack of people-skill qualities in many adults. I'm not speaking from a platform as a mother; this is in my authority as a business woman who teaches people skills as a strategy for building success and wealth. What type of people do owners hire or not hire? Who will people do business with, and who won't they do business with? Who will they vote for or not vote for?

This section is so hugely important for your children's future success.

Let me tell you that the vast majority of adults have terrible people skills. This includes those in ministry, where it is assumed that servants have great people skills and know what they are doing.

I have yet to see great people skills from teachers, lawmakers, business owners, realtors, doctors, and ministry workers, part-time as well as full-time ministers in large or small ministries. The biggest gaping hole appears in every profession, whether ministry-set or not. Anyone who trains their children to work in cooperation with other people will see their children become successful and members of the 2 percent.

We have our children read *How to Win Friends and Influence People* because every ounce of it is biblically based and reveals Christian conduct in business. Whether your position is a rocket scientist or a stay-at-home mother, every profession on the face of the planet deals with people; and the lack of people skills is the biggest point of failure in a person's life. These skills have to be taught since they don't come naturally, and parents need to set the example because their children learn from what they see them do.

1. Teach your children how to honor and respect.

Children need to honor and respect you, each other, and all human beings. This conduct will set them up for future success.

Here are examples of responses that show the opposite—dishonor and disrespect.

> "Hey listen, if you want to go to that birthday party, you need to make sure that your room is clean."
> Response: "I know, Mom!"

> "Hey, I need you to make sure to put these clothes away like this."
> Response: "I know. I know."

> "Make sure that you show up at school on time."
> Response: "Whatever."

"Make sure you get off the phone soon so you can do…"

Response: "OK, Mom! Gossshhh"

Or, the response is, "Oh God," followed by rolling eyes, drooping shoulders, and whining.

Or, there is no response at all.

All of these responses are clear examples of disrespect and dishonor, and very few parents pick up on it. I frequently hear kids talk to their parents like this and get away with it. But if *your* kids ignore what you ask them to do, then it's definitely time to teach them how to respond differently. It does not come naturally. If you're talking to them and they're ignoring you by looking around or walking away, that is utter disrespect. When you give them instructions and they run out of the room, that is disrespectful and dishonorable.

Can people succeed in life and in business without honor and respect? Can you succeed in business with "zero" people skills?

The answer is *no* to both questions. I don't care how great you, your work skills, and/or your technical skills are, if you can't work with others, you'll be unsuccessful. Here is what I know: There are no "technical" problems, there are only "people" problems. If you can figure out how to solve "people" problems, you *will* be unusually successful.

The bottom line: People skills are critically beneficial in business, marriage, and parenting. I wouldn't be where I am today if I didn't possess these skills. There's no question about that.

I don't care how great of an inventor a person is—if they don't know how to interact with people, they'll never sell that idea. I don't care how great a singer is, if she doesn't know how to market herself and get others to buy into her message and music, she'll go nowhere. If children have no honor or respect for their parents (*you!*), they'll have none for their future bosses. They'll have none for their business clients, for their spouses, or for themselves. If they're not presently treating their sisters with honor and respect, they won't treat their wives with it later. And if your daughters control, manipulate, pounce on, and boss around their brothers now, they won't be able to submit, honor, and respect their husbands later.

Look at the "big picture." You have to. If you let your children get away with less than respectful attitudes now, they will pay huge negative dividends later. Allowing them to ignore your instructions or to say, "I know," is a sure sign of an unteachable and disrespectful heart.

Don't accept sassiness, either. Teach them that a sassy attitude toward you, each other, classmates, or any human being is wrong. I've witnessed people of all ages making sassy remarks. This is seventh grade behavior, a practice that must be stopped. It is learned behavior from parents, Sunday school teachers, and friends. Little do they know that this acquired behavior hurts their identity, their future, and their success in marriage, parenting, occupation—you name it.

Tell me, would you hire someone who's teachable or unteachable? I've been in business for 20 years, and I'll tell you who I wouldn't hire—someone who comes into our office saying, "Oh, I can do that, and I've got this, and I've got that, and I'm so good at this. In fact, you are so blessed that you could meet me because if you hire me on your team, I'm telling you, I'm going to grow your company." Blah!

The one who gets the job is the same kind of person I was at 19 when I applied for a job that I was really under-qualified for. I sat with 26 other women interviewing for a custom decorating position at JCPenney's. I had "zero" decorating skills, which you could tell just by the way I dressed. I was the youngest applicant with zero education and zero experience. As the last interviewee, I sat down and said, "Mike, I want to thank you so much for giving me this opportunity. After being here, I just have to let you know I don't know a thing about decorating or colors. But if you're willing to teach me, I promise you, I will be the best decorator you've ever had. I promise you, if you're willing to take a chance on me, I will learn, and I will do anything you tell me to do."

An hour after I got home, I received a phone call, asking me if I could leave on Tuesday for four weeks of training in Seattle. "We're going to invest the next month training you."

"Yes, sir, I can! Thank you."

I was the number one decorator my first month and every single month after that. I broke the sales record in that company and made a lot of money at the age of 19. Why? Because at the very moment that counted, I was actually humble, respectful, and honest. Someone who pretends to have it all together won't go very far in life. They might be able to deceive a few, but in the long-term, it won't work. The truth comes out eventually.

Grooming my kids to be teachable, honorable, and respectful is my job.

I was sitting on an airplane a few months ago on my way to present a training seminar and two women and a little girl were sitting behind me. The little girl began crying and screaming and her mother tried bribing her, "Do you want me to get you some apple juice?"

"No, I hate apple juice!"

"OK, do you want to sit on Grandma's lap?"

"No, I hate Grandma!"

The flight attendant came around and asked, "Well, would you like something to color?"

"No, I hate coloring, and I hate you!"

The mother did nothing about this terrible behavior and speech. The little girl was allowed to say she hated her grandmother and the flight attendant—and she got away with it. In fact, she made up a song while we were about an hour into the five-hour flight, "I hate my Grandma, and I hate my Mommy, too." (This youngster sung that song because she was allowed to.) Her mother then pulled out a *Jesus Loves Me* book, and I'm thinking, *You have to be kidding me.*

Having the book suggested that the mother knew God. Yet somehow she must have missed the Scriptures pertaining to disciplining children. Where was the rod of correction that brings wisdom? I wasn't seeing it. Not only was there a lack of disciplinary measures taken, but there was also a lack of honor and respect being taught; in fact dishonor and disrespect were being taught.

This was the perfect opportunity for the mother to teach this lesson. Instead, the child was allowed to dishonor and disrespect everyone in proximity. Do you think that little girl's attitude is going to change when she starts school? Probably not. In fact, it's going to get worse. Will this child be any different when she turns 16? How about when she marries and things aren't as she likes? What's she going to do? "I hate you" is what she'll say unless some drastic intervention is made. The training from her mother reinforced her poor behavior and people skills.

Eye contact is important.

Parents, teachers, youth leaders, social workers, and anyone dealing with young people, make sure that children look you in your eyes while you're talking to them. This is something that we demand, even from a 9-month-old. They're groomed to look us in the eyes and hear what we have to say.

The first time you do this with your kids, their eyes will move all over the place. Tell them emphatically, "Look me in the eyes, and you will obey." Use the word *"obey."* It's a very powerful word that won't return void.

I look at them and demand, "Look me in the eyes, and talk to me."

That is good training, because people who can't look others in the eyes are perceived as dishonest. If you've ever been in the position of hiring and firing, would you hire someone who looks at the ground when talking to you? No way. That's one of the first things that you look for—eye contact. Is he shifty? Is she confident? It's honorable when someone looks you directly in the eyes when speaking to you.

It's dishonorable when they don't, and those in the business world will confirm this.

Can your children succeed in a future career or relationship with the opposite sex without being able to look others in the eyes? They might manipulate and bamboozle some of the people some of the time, but in the long run, this skill is a must; otherwise, they'll get a reputation for shiftiness and mistrust. Start training direct eye contact at nine months old and up. Then teach them the handshake, a very beneficial and courteous gesture that sets them up for future success. When we go places where our kids will be meeting people, I prepare them ahead of time to speak up and give a strong handshake.

2. Teach your children how to love.

Children need to be taught how to love and how to treat others the way they want to be treated. Gossiping and name-calling is not acceptable toward adults or kids. This behavior is not allowed in our home. I get down on my knees to their eye level so I'm not looking down at them, then I use a non-threatening, loving voice. My body language is disarming; it's not pushy or bullying or dishonoring. By being eye-to-eye with them, I show them that I'm honoring them, even while being in my position of authority. It is a trusting position, meant to cause them to tell the truth or not to think they have to protect themselves.

We've all heard kids say: "You're a baby!" That is name-calling and is never acceptable. It is very important to correct this conduct. This is our method of correction:

I first remind them of a Scripture we have taught them through the years which says *"Death and life are in the power of the tongue, and those who love it will eat its fruit"* (Prov. 18:21 NASB). After I have them repeat the Scripture to me, I also ask them these questions.

"Son, does it feel good to be called a *baby*? Look me in the eyes and tell me the truth."

"No, it doesn't feel good to be called a *baby*."

"Was this speaking death or life over your brother?"

He answers, "Death"

"Well, you need to apologize to your brother for calling him a *baby* because that's not honoring him. You've been trained to honor others, and you do a great job at it. But this time you made a mistake, and I am confident in the future that you will remember from this experience not to call somebody something that would make you feel bad. Instead, use your mouth to build up and encourage, as I've seen you do countless times, and I am so impressed when I see you do this. I don't want to see that kind of behavior again. Now it's time to apologize to your brother for not honoring him"

I lump everything together under a couple of key terms. One of these terms concerning people skills is **honor and/or respect**. If they've inflicted pain, hurt somebody's feelings, or wounded their spirit in any way, that is not honoring them.

I don't have them say, "I'm really sorry for calling you a baby, or stupid, or dumb." Instead, I have them say, "I'm sorry. Please, forgive me for not honoring you." By saying this, they begin to learn the definition of honor, how immensely important that word is, and begin to realize what falls under that category.

We live in a generation where honor is missing. Kids gossip about their parents and other kids constantly; children are killing classmates, their grandparents, their parents, and their school teachers. This is happening because honor and respect are not being taught in our country anymore. These qualities used to be crucial concerns in this nation, but not anymore—and our society is reaping the painful results. Please teach your children the life-changing skill of loving others.

3. Children need to be taught how to forgive and how to be forgiven.

I've been teaching and equipping tens of thousands of adults for years how to succeed in business, and can I tell you something?

Some of the biggest hindrance the majority of them have is holding bitterness, resentment, and unforgiveness against others. Why they dislike certain people or feel uncomfortable in certain situations or don't speak in public has to do with unforgiveness stemming from their childhood.

With this in mind, we groom our kids to walk in forgiveness and to reject bitterness, resentment, or taking offense against another. We don't want these spirits to take residence within them. (I encourage you to do the same.) For example, whenever I see Arika and Cabe getting edgy and showing dislike for each other, I'll say, "What just happened here?"

"Well, he did this..."

"Whoa!" I stop her right in the middle of that statement, sit them down and hold court. "Court's in session. Confession time. All right, Cabe, you're first. Tell me what *you* did to your sister. Don't tell me what she did; I want you to tell me what *you* did."

This is how to solve problems—take your kids to court. Don't fall into the misconception of asking, "OK, what did she do to you?" That's not fair, and you're teaching your child that it is OK to take no responsibility and that blame is acceptable. Let your child take full responsibility for provoking the other sibling to anger with a confession from their own mouth. Let them confess because we live in a generation of people who take no personal responsibility for their failure, but blame everybody else. Just turn on the television any time of the day or night. You'll see a variety of people who are blaming someone else for their failures.

Next, look for the fruit of forgiveness in your children's lives. If their reaction was too big for a small infraction, that signals that the fruit of bitterness and resentment is present. To correct this attitude, I teach them how to forgive one another.

(Teachers, you can use this same technique whenever you see students displaying these characteristics toward another classmate. You can guarantee that bitterness and resentment has settled in and needs to be uprooted.)

I refuse to raise more people who do not take personal responsibility for their actions!

"It was my boss. He did it."

"It was my ex-husband. He did it."

"It was my wife. She did it."

"It's my kids. If they weren't around, then I could have done this."

Whatever! These are excuses, every one of them. It's not the circumstances that determine success; it is *how we deal with circumstances that determines success.*

Groom your kids to confess with their own mouths, taking full responsibility for their actions.

> *Therefore confess your sins to each other and pray for each other so that you may be healed. The prayer of a righteous man is powerful and effective* (James 5:16).

"Cabe, what did you do to provoke your sister to this action? I don't want to hear from you what she did; I will give her a chance to make her own confessions in a minute. I want to hear what you did to provoke this reaction from her," and then he'll confess.

"Arika, what did you do to provoke your brother? I don't want to hear what he did from you. I just want to hear what you did. What was your part in this fiasco?"

Out of confession comes truth.

Groom your kids to confess their wrong; this frees them from shame and keeps their hearts clean.

Shame is a deep-rooted spirit in people that robs them from taking risks, entering relationships, or living life to its fullest. It robs people of joy and gives them guilt instead. I don't want our kids living with shame.

I want them living with pure hearts and clean hand, not carrying or covering up guilt and shame. That's what I deal with in the marketplace—adults who have been covering up their shame their entire lives.

Pornography carries the spirit of shame big-time. In the case of men or women who want to be good, do right, and walk in righteousness, if they're carrying a deeply rooted spirit of shame due to pornography, they won't tell anyone because of fear of being exposed and scorned for the rest of their lives.

No. Not in this house; there is no shame. It's called confess and get it off your chest. God forgives. If you're struggling and feeling tempted in your heart, you have to confess. This teaches children to be responsible for their own hearts and to confess so that they can be set free. They are taught not to do what 98 percent of the Church does, which is to hide their wrongdoing and not confess anything so that they can stay in bondage.

"Shame on you!"

Oftentimes parents shame their children with this common phrase that speaks shame into that child and they carry it for life. I see this in adults. I see it in 80-year-olds.

I know firsthand what that feels like. I carried that pain for a long time, and no one should have to live like that. I definitely don't want our kids living with shame.

Shame opens the door to distrust. They can't trust anybody. Then they'll begin looking for others who've been through the same situation, and this becomes the only group that they are accepted in—other shameful people. Do you wonder why kids migrate to the wrong crowd? They are carrying some kind of shame in them.

I've found that shame causes people to spend money unwisely and go deeply into debt. Everything becomes a cover-up. This opens the door to addiction because addiction is a way to cover up shame, and shameful people don't want to live with the pain of shame. Shame hurts deeply within the soul where no medicine can reach.

I see how shame operates and what it stops people from accomplishing. Many of our clients come to me with messed up marriages, kids, careers, lives, and finances because of shame. When they have been set free, I've then watched them make millions of dollars out of nowhere after struggling for 20 years. Freedom totally transforms their marriages, lives, everything!

Next, teach your children that bitterness and resentment lead to death, but forgiveness leads to freedom. They must take full responsibility!

- Have them renounce bitterness and resentment.

- Have them ask forgiveness from God for harboring bitterness and resentment.

- Have them ask each other for forgiveness.

- Have them ask for your forgiveness for doing the wrong thing and *not honoring* you.

- Teach them "*not* [to] *let the sun go down while you are still angry*" (Ephesians 4:26).

Your children need to understand that they can't change another person. We have no authority to change someone else. We have only two choices: (1) You can continue to be ticked off, hateful, and mean, or (2) You can forgive.

If children choose to forgive, then God will forgive them, and their hearts will be cleansed. At that point they'll be in a position to demonstrate to others, especially to the one who offended them, how to honor and respect others and themselves. "I'm sorry. Please forgive me for not honoring you."

[Love]...*keeps no record of wrongs* (1 Corinthians 13:5).

Children have to be taught to live in forgiveness. They have to learn to apologize and make things right. "I'm sorry. Please, forgive me, I was wrong."

Whatever the infraction, I have our children apologize and make it right by confessing with their own mouths. We, as parents or the adult influence, must also do the same thing when we makes mistakes. I've apologized countless times to our children when I've misunderstood, responded incorrectly, or dishonored them in some way. I've humbled myself face-to-face, eye-to-eye, apologizing and asking their forgiveness.

I've set the example for them because even we, as the parent or adult influence, have messed up, misjudged, misunderstood, or didn't communicate clearly. We need to fess up and lead these young people by example. If you do, then you've proven to them that you are a person they can trust. Otherwise, you're portrayed as a dictator, perfect and righteous, and they're nothing but wrong. This attitude won't build trust between you and your kids. Remember, we live in a generation that blames and doesn't take responsibility, so we have to model the exact opposite for our children.

4. To develop leadership qualities, children need to know how to follow a leader.

The best leaders were once great followers. I still have coaches that I follow, and I have people who follow me by the thousands. As I've learned to lead, I'm leading others.

Teach your children that they are leading right now in some ways, but they need to become great followers before they can ever become great leaders. Also, teach them how to follow the right kind of people, meaning their parents first, their teachers next. Make sure your children know what is right, because if they don't, then they can be led to slaughter.

Teach them to honor their coaches, teachers, and the rest of the authorities in their lives with "yes, sir" or "yes, ma'am." By honoring the coach, they are leading by example and will stand out from the crowd. We remind them that they are not trying to gain points with their teammates or classmates. That is not the focus.

The focus is to honor their coach or teacher and follow their leadership. When they follow their directions, work with the spirit of excellence, and have a respectful attitude in all that they do, God will prosper the work of their hands.

For example, Arika loves little kids. She has always had favor with younger kids. She has been all over the world on mission trips working with kids since she was 11. When she returned from one of these trips, she didn't have much patience for her brothers.

"This is a test, Arika. If you don't lead your brothers well, how will God trust you to lead other people's kids? This is your training ground right here and right now."

Then I talked with her brothers about them not following their older sister's directions when she was acting on our authority. We may have told her to tell them to put the dishes away and they rebelled, giving her attitude or saying, "Gosh, Arika."

"Boys, some day you're going to lead a family for sure. You're becoming a leader of a home or a business or a state as a politician. You may be a coach leading a hockey or basketball team. Someday as a young man you will lead, but in order to be a great leader, you first must learn how to follow and follow well. If you can be trusted following your sister's directions, then God can trust you to lead others. But if you can't be trusted to follow directions that your sister is giving you on our authority, then you'll certainly not be able to lead well in the future."

Then I'll encourage them.

"I know and I'm confident that you are able to follow directions and follow them well. I've seen you do this countless times, and I feel so good when I see you with a smile on your face, Micah, following directions when you're cleaning the stove or helping out in the yard. Man, I've watched you work with a spirit of excellence, honoring your sister with a smile on your face and a hop in your step. I know that you can do it, and you can do it well. What God is training you to do right now is to someday honor the wife and daughters that will be living in your home and the female co-workers working with you in whatever career you have. I know that you have the ability to do it; now I want you to do it and do it right."

If they had an infraction with their sister and wouldn't honor or follow her correctly, then I made them apologize right then and there.

"Please forgive me, Arika, for not honoring you."

Honor works both ways.

If our sons are mouthy to their sister, how will they treat other women in their lives? If I allow them to be mouthy to me, how will they treat their future wives and daughters or future female bosses? If they are allowed to be mouthy to their women teachers, I am setting them up to fail in the future when they have to work or live with women. And guess what? They will have to do both of these things. They are going to have to deal with women for the rest of their lives, and if I let them get away with not following directions from their sister, female teacher, or mother, I am teaching our sons to dishonor other humans (and females in particular), and that is wrong. It sets them up for a future divorce. It sets them up to get fired; it sets them up for failure.

I have five children, so someone is always leading someone. Here's a prime example. I met with our son's teacher recently and was told, "Roman really has a lot of influence over the class."

I asked, "Do you want to use that to your benefit?"

"Well, sure I do," the teacher said.

"Pull him aside and say, 'Roman, I want to be able to get the kids to work on this particular project. Is there any way you can help me to get everyone to cooperate so that we can get the project done quickly? If we can get it done quickly, we can play this game...'"

The teacher looked at me and said, "Oh my gosh!" After using this technique, she now has much more control over her class than before. Since identifying leadership qualities in our son, he now leads that class. When she needs something done, all she has to do is bring him in and make her request, and he does it because he's got influence. When he was younger, I groomed him about the power of influence that he possessed and that it was his choice to influence them to do well or not so well.

There are plenty of scenarios to use to demonstrate principles for our kids. These scenarios are a dime a dozen, especially bad ones that depict negativity.

Paint a picture.

Cabe at one point said he wanted to be a hockey coach. I asked why and he said he liked helping others to do well and liked making an impact on their lives. Now I consistently use his goal as a hockey coach to paint a picture for him concerning other people.

"Cabe, you said that you want to have an impact on a lot of people's lives. That's influence. Cabe, can you help me out? We need to get the kitchen clean, and we can either do it quickly or slowly. We can do it with whining or with joy. Which do you choose?"

"With joy, and fast," he answers.

"Great! Would you be willing to help me motivate your brothers to work with a good attitude and a spirit of excellence?"

"Sure Mom!"

See, Cabe is a pot-stirrer. He's a motivator; so my job is to motivate him in the right direction instead of allowing him to pull his brother's ear when trying to get something done. That prevents fighting in the kitchen. I preempt his natural tendencies and direct him to want to do well instead of wanting to do badly. This prepares him for his role as a future husband, positively motivating his family and leading the household. If he does become a hockey coach in the future, he'll be prepared to lead correctly. The truth is that every man leads something and someone.

For instance, I'll say, "OK, if we get it done fast, then you can go outside and play longer."

This makes him go yelling to his brothers, "Hey, guys! Guess what? We've got a chance to help Mom in the kitchen, and if we get it done quickly, then we'll be able to go outside and play longer."

They'll answer, "OK, Cabe."

I taught them to honor Cabe, their older brother, who was 11 at that time. This was their opportunity to honor a higher position and be great followers. This is also Cabe's opportunity to be a great leader. This taught him a valuable lesson about influence and its effect on others, and I groomed this early in him and his brothers.

Now he's developed a gift of influence. Someday this quality will help him lead a corporation or a congregation. Someday this quality may lead a nation.

5. Teach them not to argue.

God taught me this fact through watching business people argue. Adults take business right out of their hands by arguing with their clients, team members, and even prospective new clients. I've seen this. Arguing with the marketplace will cause you to lose. It's just that simple. Argue with your client, and your client will find somebody else to do business with.

Remember the Scripture I mentioned earlier: *Do everything without complaining and arguing.* I've come across more adult whiners and complainers than anybody else in my life. They want to make it and become super successful, but instead they whine, get no results, and give a bunch of excuses.

"If only the company would give us the deal on this."

"I don't know why, but I always seem to find people who are broke."

"My husband doesn't support me."

"I just don't get enough help."

"I don't know what's wrong, but I always find advertisers that can't really get the job done."

"Wah…wah…wah!"

If there's anything that drives me crazy, it's whining and complaining. I can't stand it. And why do we have so many whiners and complainers? Because someone's parent let them whine and complain, that's why. Because someone's parent somewhere down the road just overlooked their bad behavior.

"No big deal. Oh, well. That's just what kids do."

That's *not* what our kids do! Our kids aren't allowed to. That's a standard we set, an environment we live in. This is how I figured out how to groom kids. It's better to teach them when they are young not to argue and complain. *"Do everything without complaining and arguing."*

I had a revelation one day that a 9-month-old who is whining is actually complaining, so I taught our kids sign language when they were as young as 9 months. Whether it was "more please" or "all done," they learned how to communicate without words because I refused to let them whine.

Don't argue with a kid.

A woman who helped with our kids was arguing with our 9-year-old son one day. I looked at her and said, "Do you realize that you're arguing with a 9-year-old?"

This is arguing with a child:

- When you give instructions to a 9-year-old and he says, "Oh, man!" And then you say, "Listen buddy, you've got to get that done because of dah-dah-dah-dah-dah!"

- If you're reasoning with a 9-year-old after you've given the instructions, "Go upstairs and clean your room. I'm giving you 15 minutes to do it," and he says, "I don't want to!" and you say, "I don't care if you don't want to. Here's the deal, we've got to do this and that."

This is what I said to her, "I've trained our son that arguing and complaining is unacceptable. Now you are setting another standard that says arguing is: number one, allowed, and number two, acceptable to disrespect a woman.

"I don't want you to teach our son how to disrespect his future wife. So please, don't argue with him. This is what you should say: 'Cabe, go upstairs and clean your room.' If he gives you one of these, 'Well, gosh!' say, 'Would you like to try that again? I'd like to see you succeed and not get yourself into trouble.'"

For me, if I catch our kids trying to enter into an arguing or complaining stint (whether it's putting the dishes away, picking up toys, or whatever is grooming them to be responsible and respectful) and they say, "Oh, man!" my response is always, "Would you like to try that again?"

Don't allow a sad disposition.

I have one child who is very emotional and expressive; he thinks with his mouth, not his mind. I'll say, "Would you like to try that again?"

"Yes, Mom!" he'll answer sadly, his shoulders shrugged, his back out of whack and his arms nearly touching his knees. (I've seen adults do the same thing. In fact, I've done it. Maybe you have, too.)

I'll look at him and say, "Look me in the eyes. I want to help you succeed. Roman, do you want to try that again, this time choosing joy?"

He'll take a deep breath, "Yes, Mom."

"Awesome job, buddy! High-five!" and he'll willingly go upstairs to do the job that I asked him to do.

Do you understand? Attitudes are everything when it comes to success. If you allow your kids to choose sadness, worry, fret, and ungratefulness, then you're grooming those attitudes in them. You're grooming them to be unsuccessful and to end up divorced because who the heck can live with that crap? No one can. Who can live with a sad, pathetic, weepy, and mopey attitude? "Wah...wah...wah! Poor me! Everything's so bad!"

No one wants to live with that. No one can stand it.

Our son, the emotional one, has to be groomed from this attitude. I'll say to him, "Roman, you've told Mommy that you love people and that you love to be around friends. Mommy wants to help you have a lot of them, and this sad, mopey, wah-wah-wah thing, people don't want to be around people like that. If you want a lot of friends, you've got to choose joy, because people love enthusiasm. They love smiles and great attitudes. So what are you going to choose? Are you going to choose life or death, joy or sadness?"

"I choose life!" he says. He's so funny. And now, it's a keyword. It's branded.

"Roman, what are you going to choose?"

"Life!" He may be sad at that moment, but in an instant, his state of mind changes. "I choose life!"

Attitude is everything. You know that. Maybe you struggle in business because you've chosen death and have an attitude of ungratefulness. You've chosen to see only what's bad, negative, wrong, horrible, and what's not working.

You must groom your kids, and yourself, to see the good in a bad situation. Groom them, and yourself, to be hopeful, to seek out what's right and good and noble and pure, and choose joy instead of sadness. You have to groom them to do that.

Imagine if your parents groomed you that way. Come on, think about it. Can you imagine yourself being groomed in this manner? No doubt it would have made quite a difference.

6. *Gossip versus encouragement.*

Calling people names should not be allowed. Let me tell you why. Name-calling is a seed for gossip, and gossipers don't get promoted in business or in life. Gossip in a marriage means the destruction of that marriage. Gossip from children of the household is mutiny among the children and the parents. Teach your children how to encourage instead. We taught our children to *"encourage one another and build each other up"* (1 Thess. 5:11).

A forked tongue will prevent your children from being trusted by anyone and will keep them from getting a job and keeping a job. It will prevent them from being promoted in any career. A forked tongue is unacceptable, disrespectful, and dishonorable, and it destroys the gossiper's confidence.

Teach them this lesson early in life. *Scare the pants off them!* Share with them that the greatest law of success is the Law of Sowing and Reaping. So if you're sowing gossip, a harvest-full of people will gossip about you at some point in your life.

Stop gossip in a heartbeat.

"Gossip is not acceptable. That is not for this family to do. This family is set apart for success. We will not be like the 98-percenters who sit around gossiping about other people's lives. The Bible says not to let one idle word come out of our mouths because we will be judged for it, so make every word count.

"What do you want your reputation to be, son or daughter? Do you want to be known as someone who can't be trusted because you're a gossiper? I know what God has set you apart to be—someone who can be trusted."

I just recently had this conversation with Roman.

"I deal with adults every day, and I hear confessions by the thousands. I know some of the deepest, darkest secrets about people, and they trust that I won't reveal them to anyone else. You will be trustworthy for others, as well.

"I've heard men as old as 65 confess that some boy in the 4th grade made a horrible comment that hurt them badly for the rest of their lives. Then I walk them through a process of forgiveness for what they've held on to and unsuccessfully tried to fight for 55 or more years.

"There will come a day, Roman, when all the friends around you will give you a reputation for being either mean to them or nice. You get to choose what reputation will follow you long after you're out of school."

Then, in order to motivate him, I gave him a biblical reputation to want to live up to. (I learned this from *How to Win Friends and Influence People*.)

"You will stand out in somebody's mind someday and either it will be negative or positive. You have a chance, now, to show good or evil through the life of Roman. One or the other, you have to make one choice."

I can't believe what this talk did in Roman. The results were phenomenal.

Children should be encouraging and build each other up.

I tell them, "Guys, out there you're going to find people who want to trip you. They want to hurt you, and they're going to be mean to you. But guess what? That's called 'life.' That's why, as a family, we have to stick together and buoy each other up. As a family, we have to spur each other on. As a family, we have to encourage each other to take those risks and be all that we can be. We have to do that for each other."

Imagine if you were groomed as a child to see the good in others instead of the bad. I'm an encourager. I wasn't intentionally groomed to be one, but out of rebellion against the discouragement in my household, I became an encouragement. This is why people call me their best friend and have named their children after me.

CHAPTER 8

STRATEGY #4:
CORRECTION & ACCOUNTABILITY

Whoever loves discipline loves knowledge, but he
who hates correction is stupid.
—Proverbs 12:1

DON'T BE AFRAID TO CORRECT OR
HOLD YOUR KIDS ACCOUNTABLE!

Some of you have great concerns regarding discipline, but children desperately need discipline. Correction and accountability is very much needed in the *next generation*. This is an important topic and probably the most controversial subject discussed in this book.

Coming from an abusive home, I certainly had a big concern about discipline when it came to my children. My abusive stepfather kicked us, picked us up and threw us across the room, and held us against the walls by our throats. My sisters and I, even our mother, often had black eyes and bruises all over our bodies. When people grow up the way I did, one of two things will happen when they have their own families:

1.   They don't discipline at all, or

2.   They discipline in the same manner they were disciplined, which was out of anger.

I believe that God disciplines those He loves. (See Hebrews 12:6.) I believe that there is a right way and a wrong way to discipline; the right way is in love and the wrong way is in anger. The right way to discipline is not beating or provoking children to hate you for disciplining them.

The Bible says that a person who hates correction will have destruction in their path.

> *Stern discipline awaits him who leaves the path; he who hates correction will die* (Proverbs 15:10).

> *A fool spurns his father's discipline, but whoever heeds correction shows prudence* (Proverbs 15:5).

A man or woman with pride cannot handle being corrected, and they will never succeed in anything.

> *Pride only breeds quarrels, but wisdom is found in those who take advice* (Proverbs 13:10).

Speak with authority when grooming this skill. Let it be laced with love; not as a dictator, but under this authority: "I'm here for you to succeed. I'm here to gird you up so you can be the best that you can be, and that is a good boy or girl." Tell them this, but *never* tell them that they are *bad*.

I've personally lead thousands through deep inner healing, and when I get to the bottom or the root of the issue, many will begin to cry and say, "I'm a *bad* boy" (or girl)." It's a statement that they haven't heard themselves called in 30 years, but it was a seed that was planted within them and it wounded their spirit. If you've called your son or daughter *bad*, please ask for their forgiveness. Tell them that they're a *good* little boy or girl, that God loves them, that you love them, and that they just made a *bad* choice. Discipline the action; don't tear down the individual. Don't hurt them by speaking death over them. Condemn the choice they made, not the person.

I believe in first-time obedience. I believe in this fully. Obeying on the fourth or fifth time is not an option with me.

FOUR TYPES OF OBEDIENCE

1. **Reluctant obedience**. This is when you have to be pushed to do something. There's reluctance within that says, "I don't know if I want to. I'm just not sure." That's reluctance. Just like I tell my children, I'm going to tell you, there's no blessing with reluctant obedience. In fact, there is no reward for reluctant obedience

2. **Grudging obedience**. "Fine, I'll do it! I don't want to, and I don't like it, but I'll do it." If you have children, then you have heard them respond like this. This is rebellion, not obedience, and it comes with a curse. Reluctant obedience and grudging obedience cause stress. It causes destiny to be prolonged. It causes hardship, headaches, and division; that's the fulfillment of the curse.

3. **Willing obedience**. I was the worst with obedience. *Obedience* was like a curse word; I would only obey Hans as a martyr. "OK, fine! I'll do it," but inside I'd be saying, "NO!" I would obey, but I'd obey unwillingly and with a grudge—that does *not* get a blessing! There's a blessing that comes with being willing to obey. I eventually realized the importance of willingly obeying.

4. **Fully abandoned, fully surrendered obedience**. With the willing obedience that I'd experienced, there was still fear and no guarantees; I was just going to trust. Even though I was still afraid to be willingly obedient, I would do it. I'd push down the grudge, push away the reluctance, and willingly obey, still afraid and still not fully trusting. But then I came to a place of fully abandoned, fully surrendered obedience with no guarantee of any result. This is what Christ exemplified on the cross, a fully surrendered obedience to redeem your life and mine. There is a great blessing, and it honors God for us to fully surrender with full abandonment and absolutely no guarantees.

Obeying the first time is important for success!

I constantly come in contact with business people who won't follow directions. Because they don't obey, they fail. They refuse to follow directions, are not teachable, and are constantly pushing the envelope to reinvent the wheel their own way. The vast majority of these kinds of people fail. They can't keep a job, and they have very little stability. They can't succeed in business because they're unteachable and they're forever looking for the greener grass, always chasing the wind.

Again, this is not my opinion as a mother. This is my opinion as a business woman who has coached tens of thousands of people and hired many employees. I have seen those who succeed and those who fail. People who cannot follow directions get fired. It's that simple. They may have the best intentions, but the bottom line: if they can't get it done, they will have to find somewhere else to go. Rather than alleviating stress, they are adding to it. Do you want your son or daughter to be known as dependable and reliable or undependable and unreliable?

I recognized this principle before I began raising kids. I vowed to *groom my kids to obey, follow directions, and to follow through the first time I tell them something. This way, I'll be grooming them for success.*

Imagine being trained as a child in this manner—follow directions the first time; hear a request and follow through immediately when instructions were given. If you are struggling with procrastination, you weren't groomed to obey the first time. You were groomed to obey the seventh time.

James Dobson wrote a book titled *Dare to Discipline*. I encourage you to read it. I read it about 10 years ago, and it really made a powerful impact on me and many other people. This book was recommended by a family member who had great success using it. Another great program is a tape series called Preparation for Parenting, *which has an awesome program for newborns. It saved my sanity with my last two babies,* and it suggests a great plan for having your baby on a schedule as well as a number of other tips that will prepare you for the transitions that come with a newborn baby. Our programs differ in that theirs don't teach how to *groom your kids for success. These programs have great information and are helpful.*

After studying about discipline for many years, I believe that the best approach is to discipline when there is *deliberate disobedience.* When disciplining, we use the following four powerful, scriptural words: obey, self-control, patience, and honor.

1. **Obey.** Look into their eyes, and say, "Obey!" This even works with two-year-olds. They'll say, "OK!"

2. **Self-control.** Here's a prime example. Our son went running through the kitchen after I had just cleaned the sliding glass door, which was a rarity. He thought the door was open, so he kept running. He hit it and fell down screaming; his lips turned blue. I looked at him, pointed and said, *"self-control."* The screaming stopped in-

stantly. I can't tell you how many times I've done this—hundreds of time because I have a lot of kids. Every time they hurt themselves, I look at them and say, "self-control."

Have you been in a public place where a kid is screaming at the top of their lungs because of something that happened or because they didn't get their way? (Ha! I've even done this to other people's kids and to my goddaughters when they've been totally manipulating the heck out of their parents.) I look at them and say, "self-control." Boom! Mouths shut.

Micah, who's now 10, had what we called a "one-eyed cry" when he was very young (around 9 months old). "Wah!" One eye would remain open to see if anyone was watching. This was the signal for us to know if he was faking. The one-eyed cry meant nothing but drama, that he was simply looking for attention and learning to manipulate us. The two-eyed cry was genuine, but 99 percent of the time, he cried a one-eyed cry.

This proved to me that babies are very aware and conscious of what they are doing at a very young age. They know how to manipulate, control, and get our attention. If screaming gets our attention, then they scream. You will have to learn to discern a real cry from a manipulative one. For Micah, his one-eyed cry was an alert for us. When I saw it, I'd say, "Ooh, that's a one-eyed cry. I'm not responding to that." Either way, using the words "self-control" stops the crying, whether it's a one-eyed cry or a two-eyed cry.

I use the words "self-control" even if they have a bone sticking out. In fact, a couple of years ago, Roman decided to take a skateboard with no wheels down a dirt hill and—boom—fell right on his elbow and broke it. He screamed! This son of mine has a voice and a mouth that's bigger than mine. I looked at him and said, "Self-control, Roman." I knew it was hard for him to control the crying because he literally broke his elbow. "Self-control Roman, look at me! Crying that bad is going to make it hurt more. Do you want it to feel better?"

"Yes, Mommy." he answered.

"OK, self-control." Do you know our little guy just whimpered in the back of the truck the whole way to the hospital—just whimpered for 25 minutes. He couldn't stop whimpering, which is how we knew something was really wrong, but he stopped screaming his brains out and calmed down with that command.

Isn't that awesome? It works. Use it today, please. Don't allow another kid to scream their guts out in public again. This is how hypochondriacs are groomed; they are groomed when you buckle in and coddle the drama. Bring them into alignment instead. Move them from hysterics into reality; into what's acceptable, well-balanced, and healthy.

When we respond to their hysterics and their drama, they learn how to manipulate your attention. They'll discover how to push your buttons to make you pay attention to them, and guess what? They'll use that in high school, college, and as an adult. They'll learn that if they get hysterical, you'll put up the money. Don't groom them to manipulate you. Instead, groom them on what you know is best for their future.

3. **Patience.** There's always going to be a 2-year-old or a 16-year-old who wants to interrupt when you're talking to somebody else. Their need is urgent to them and something that they must do *now*. This is how you should respond:

    "Can you be patient?" I've done this to a 1-year-old and even they understand, for some reason. I don't know why, but I believe it's because the Word of God is in them. When I say, "Can you be patient," they look at me, nod their heads, and wait patiently.

    I've taught our kids that interrupting is not honorable. If yours are doing this, then you need to correct this activity because it shows poor people skills. Groom them while they're young, so that when they're older, it's easy for them to use this skill.

    To encourage this skill, I've taught our kids to put their hand on my arm and to keep it there. This gives me a signal, so when I have a break in communications with an adult, I'll say, "Can you excuse me one minute?" Then I'll address our child, "OK, what can I help you with?" Then, they're allowed to speak.

    Until they get this in their minds, I'll continue to do this every time they interrupt me. "You're

interrupting; do what we have taught you to do."
I'll take their hand, place it on my arm, and say,
"OK, can you be patient?"

"Yes."

Then, I'll finish the conversation which might
take another two to five minutes, and they just sit
there waiting for my attention. Then I'll say, "OK,
what can I help you with?" That's honorable. It
works with 1-year-olds. It works with teenagers. I
promise you, it works. Use it!

4. **Honor.** In the People Skill strategy, I mentioned
    the importance of honor and demonstrating it to
    your children by your example of honoring them.
    If you want honor, then you have to give honor.
    You honor them by confessing your mistakes to
    them. You honor them by preparing them for the
    next environment they are about to enter and the
    proper responses.

    Your children honor you when they follow
    your directions, when they are obedient and
    respond the first time without arguing and
    complaining.

CORRECTION & ACCOUNTABILITY

We use the *Encourage-Correct-Encourage* system when disciplining our children (we use a very similar approach with our employees and clients that we coach). It sets them up for success by assuring
them that loving discipline is necessary to correct unwanted behavior.
As a result, they understand that our love for them and our concern
for their future compel us to train them with the necessary skills for

the way that they should go. This is how we equip them for a successful future in life.

DISCIPLINE—DELIBERATE DISOBEDIENCE

Deliberate disobedience always gets a spanking. Some of you
will have a hard time with this, but let me point you to this Scripture:
*Folly is bound up in the heart of a child, but the rod of discipline will
drive it far from him* (Prov. 22:15). The discipline that God is talking
about is loving discipline that leads to success. It is not because you're
mad at your children. It's not in anger, although there are times God
disciplines us for ticking Him off real good with idolatry and other
disobedient deeds.

This is the foundation for loving discipline that's based on
Scripture.

> *Do not withhold discipline from a child; if you punish
> him with the rod, he will not die* (Proverbs 23:13).

> *The rod of correction imparts wisdom, but a child left
> to himself disgraces his mother* (Proverbs 29:15).

> *Discipline your son, and he will give you peace; he will
> bring delight to your soul* (Proverbs 29:17).

> *He who spares the rod hates his son, but he who loves
> him is careful to discipline him* (Proverbs 13:24).

This is good stuff even if you don't believe in the Bible. (Just
pretend I didn't say it was from the Bible if you can't handle it.)
There are some who have psychoanalyzed these Scriptures and
think the *rod* means something different. Think what you want,

but I can bet that you've never read the whole Bible cover-to-cover. When you do read it cover-to-cover, you will find out exactly how He disciplines those He loves. Quite honestly, the *rod* was very minor and soft compared to other forms of discipline that God brings on those He loves.

So if you don't think that the *rod* meant rod, then you don't know Him. You also don't know how serious He is about obedience. Obedience took Christ to the cross. First-time obedience will enable you to fulfill your destiny in life. Argue if you want about whether it was a stick, branch, or whatever. All I know is that I spanked our kids with a spoon or a belt, and when they reached age 6 and older, I rarely had to discipline in that manner again. Now it's once a year maybe for some of our kids, or once every three years or almost never for the others. Just saying, "Do you want to try that again?" sends shivers up their spine and snaps them to attention.

An example of deliberate disobedience:

"Please do not pick that up!" and they pick it up anyway. This calls for an immediate spanking. When a rule is established and they know it's a rule but disobey anyway, that's deliberate disobedience.

Say, "This is deliberate disobedience, and for that, there is discipline."

Make sure that they understand why they're being disciplined. Let them know that it's not for writing on the walls or picking up what they were told not to pick up—it's for *deliberate disobedience.* You will confuse your children if you point out everything they do wrong. Just lump it all under one category, instead. Ah! Now they're learning the meaning of *deliberate disobedience* and not the *act* of writing on the walls.

"Did Mommy tell you that writing on the wall is not acceptable?"

"Yes."

"So, that means you deliberately disobeyed and wrote on the wall."

"Yes."

"So, that means discipline for deliberate disobedience."

There's a psychological process that children go through in understanding that *deliberate disobedience* is not good. If you discipline them for writing on the walls and say, "I'm spanking you because you wrote on the wall," well, think about it. They'll probably never write on the walls again, and how does that groom them for future success? As they mature and become adults, they won't write on the wall. When they're adults, they won't say, "Oh, I'm going to play with that toy anyway." There's a giant gap between how a child and an adult thinks, but both can understand the words that I've given you. Obedience is an adult concept, as well as a childhood concept. So we have to teach them how to lovingly and willingly obey.

I want our kids to understand that *deliberate disobedience* calls for *discipline*. As an adult, when their boss says, "I want X, Y, Z done at this time." It would be deliberate disobedience if they answered, "I don't care if you want it done at this time or not. I'm not doing it." That's *deliberate disobedience*. Instead, a spirit of conviction will rise up in them, saying, "Oh, I better do that. I better obey." Understand?

Lump every act of defiance under *deliberate disobedience*. Lying, cheating, and stealing always get corrected with a spanking because they are under the deliberate disobedience category. Why? Because you've groomed them not to do those things, if they do it anyway, they deliberately did it and tried to get away with it. This is *deliberate disobedience*—boom! Take care of it the first time around. Maybe they didn't know it was wrong. Maybe you didn't explain it clearly.

Say: "Listen, you may not have known that's called stealing. But I'm going to tell you right now that it's stealing, and if you ever do that again, that's *deliberate disobedience*. Now I'm confident that you want to do the right thing, as you've done many times before. The good boy that you are, Micah, wants to do the right thing. So I'm sure that you will stay away from anything that even looks close to stealing."

This is giving them a reputation that they will want to choose and reminding them of how good they've been in the past. This is in stark contrast to reminding them of their past failures.

Don't say:

- "This is the third time you've done that!"

- "Why are you always getting yourself into trouble?"

- "How many times do I have to tell you?"

Never say those things to your kids, *never*. A parent who speaks like this is revealing their frustration and the fact that they're keeping a record of wrong and have not forgiven the children. If you continue to do this, you will become unsafe to your children, and they will not trust you.

Instead, always remind them of their successes and the good choices that they've made in the past. Let them know that you believe in them and have confidence that this won't happen again. Let them know that this infraction was out of character for them, and then point them in the right direction. Restore their identity in the goodness that God has done in them.

I've watched parents roll their eyes at their kids, storm out of rooms, slam doors, and do everything that they instruct their kids not to do. These parents are acting exactly like their kids, and then they can't understand why their kids have no respect for them.

Quit acting like your kids. That might be the first place to start regaining their respect. Rolling your eyes at your teenager will not work. It's displaying a disrespectful attitude, plus you've taught them that this is an acceptable way to act at any age.

This is important because kids will do what they see even more so than listen to what you're saying. So if you've acted in this manner, you have no credibility to stand on, and you need to make it right. Say to your kids, "I'm sorry. Please forgive me. I've really messed that up, and I've set a terrible example for you. We're both going to have to work on this." This will restore your credibility and their trust in you.

DISCIPLINE—DISRESPECTFUL ATTITUDE

Always discipline an attitude of disrespect.

Correct it verbally!
"Do you want to try that again?"

"No, I don't want to."

"Well, now, you've crossed the line into *deliberate disobedience*. (That is the key word for spanking. This is not a warning. Instantly, I have their attention.) Are you sure you want to go down this road, or would you like to try that again?"

"Yes, Mom, I'd be glad to try that again." (That's usually the answer I receive when we get to this point and the answer I'm looking for.)

Words are powerful, and they have triggers in the mind. When they've been trained to believe that deliberate disobedience equals ouch, and ouch is not what they want, they will shape up fast and give you the correct attitude, especially when they're older.

If they refuse, the attitude is corrected with a spanking.
"OK, I'm sorry you chose the other way. We will have to discipline you because of deliberate disobedience."

Correct how they treat others with a verbal correction.
This includes bickering, arguing, and complaining.
*Give a **warning***!

- Warn them about attitudes.

- Warn them about disrespect.

- Encourage and speak life in the direction they
  can go and have chosen before.

That's why I asked, "You want to try that again?" That's a warning.

"OK, if you continue in this direction, that's *deliberate disobedience*, and you know how we have to take care of that."

DISCIPLINE—FOR YOUNG KIDS

All right, here's a quick formula and then we're done with this subject. For kids under 12 this is our discipline technique.

- Explain why they're being spanked.

- Depending on their age, have them tell you why
  they're being disciplined.

I ask, "Tell mommy why we need to discipline you?"

Notice I never use the word *spank*. As adults they won't be spanked, but they will be disciplined. The world will discipline them, the system will discipline them, and God will discipline them. You want them to get the wisdom about discipline early on.

I say, "OK, explain to me why you're being disciplined."

After they speak, then decide whether to use a leather belt or a spoon. (Again, I know some of you were abused as a kid. So was I. This used to be very difficult for me to do, but now I'm a healthy mom who wants to see her kids groomed for success.) Because of my love for our kids, I won't spare the rod because I don't want spoiled children. I don't want children who will lead their own lives into folly, which is what we're seeing nationwide right now (kids being raised by daycare workers with zero discipline). No discipline, no wisdom. I want the men and women I'm raising in our home to be wise, so I give three swats with a spoon or a belt (a rod of correction.)

- Next, I hug and I encourage them.

- Then, if there was a squabble between them, I have them ask forgiveness of each other; forgiveness from me for dishonoring me by disobeying me; and forgiveness from God.

This is what you'll find as you complete this step. Sometimes the swat doesn't mean a thing. I have one child and the swat doesn't mean anything to him. But as soon as he has to confess and ask forgiveness, that's when he breaks. His heart softens and he's just "so sorry." This is when his heart transforms, when he has to bow his head and ask God to forgive him for what he's done. That's the place where he cracks, always. And this is what you're looking for. You're looking for a heart change in the action.

Our fourth baby was that way. He rebelled against any kind of correction. As soon as the correction happened, he'd be mad. But when he had to confess and ask forgiveness of me or God—oh! That's when his heart broke at his misdeeds.

The good news is that you will find that as they get older you will rarely have to physically discipline them, if ever. With mine, like

I said before, from 6 years old and up, our kids rarely get into enough trouble for a spanking. They respond very quickly to the verbal warning, which triggers an alert in their brain.

Deliberate disobedience will hurt them now and in their future, and that's a fact.

> *But if anyone causes one of these little ones who believe in me to sin, it would be better for him to have a large **millstone** hung around his neck and to be drowned in the depths of the sea. Woe to the world because of the things that cause people to sin! Such things must come, but woe to the man through whom they come!* (Matthew 18:6-7)

Not disciplining your children for their disobedience misleads a child and sets them up for failure. It sets them up for physical, mental, emotional, spiritual, and financial failures. People who think that there is no discipline for disobedience have their heads in the sand and are living in a dream world compared to the one we actually live in. Reality check! According to the laws we live under, if you disobey, you're going to pay. What you sow you reap.

We are totally misleading our kids if we don't discipline them for their actions.

SCENARIO

Your precious little one has been told once already that writing on the walls is not acceptable. He chose to do it anyway.

"You know what, son? I need to discipline you because you deliberately disobeyed by writing on the walls. So, tell me, why did you choose to be disciplined?"

"…because I wrote on the walls."

"OK, no. That's not why. It's because you disobeyed."

"OK, because I disobeyed."

"OK, turn over and close your eyes." I have him close his eyes so he's basically hugging the bed, then I swat three times, turn him back over, hug him and hold him tight. Then, I encourage him, and ask, "Are you a good boy?"

"Yes, Mommy; I'm a good boy."

"Do you know that your Mommy loves you?"

"Yes."

"Who else loves you?"

"Daddy loves me."

"Who else?"

"My brothers and my sisters love me."

"Who else?"

"God loves me."

"Yes, and does God want to see you succeed?"

"Yes."

"This is why He put me in your life, to help you to succeed. Can you see if I let you keep doing this, it's only going to hurt your future?"

"Yes."

"OK. So what are you going to do?"

"I'm going to do better next time. I will obey."

"OK. What do you need to say to me?" (And again I'd correct their attitude immediately, even if we're in public.) Every time they get corrected, I ask the same question, "What do you need to say to me?"

"Mommy, please forgive me for not obeying you."

I don't care if they were disrespectful at a restaurant, a grocery store, or any public spot, I stop and deal with it right there on the spot. If not, then they figure it's all right to disobey me there. I ask, "What do you need to say to me?"

"Mommy, please forgive me for disrespecting or not honoring you."

When our kids were little, I would tell them that I was wearing a belt and that the truck is over there. "I will take you to that truck and give what you need. So you have a choice to make right now. Either you are going to shape up and follow what you know is right, or you're going to disobey. Which one is it going to be?" Then I say this with a smile, "I'd much rather see you succeed."

If they were in cahoots with somebody else or they hurt somebody else, they'd have to ask that person and God to forgive them. We live in a world where most people take no responsibility for their actions. But as soon as they start taking responsibility—oh, my gosh—they're going to succeed.

Taking no responsibility leads to blame; this is the voice of a victim. Victims have few relationships and don't succeed in life. Thus the number one drug prescribed in America today is antidepressants. We live in a blaming, victimized, take-no-responsibility society. Turn on the television any time of day within the last 20 years and you'll see the same thing—people blaming others for their current life of despair. It's a rare breed of people who actually do take responsibility, and these are the ones who will make true, lasting changes in their lives. These are the ones who will succeed.

DISCIPLINE—FOR OLDER KIDS

With 13 years and up, I use the same words, but I also take something away from them. Take a privilege or dessert away, a movie, their phone privileges, or the computer. Whatever it is that they love (sports activities, youth group activities, hanging with their friends) have them sacrifice it. Then if everything has been taken away, add chores. Oftentimes when kids are getting in trouble, it's because they are bored.

The rest of the formula is the same as with younger children:

- "Why are we disciplining you?"

- "What do you need to say to me?"

- "Now, what do you need to say to God?"

- "This is the action that we're going to have to take," or "What kind of action do you think we should take?"

- "You are an awesome young man [or woman] and I'm confident that you will make better choices in the future, as I've seen you do most of your life." (End with a positive statement, speaking life over them.)

Make sure your children take full responsibility for the disciplining that's going on. That's called correction and accountability.

Many have failed in business because of a lack of correction and accountability, yet *anyone who rejects correction is totally leading themselves down a road of destruction.* If we don't take heed and train our kids while young, as adults they will refuse to receive correction. And if they refuse correction, they cannot be mentored or coached. They will never become an apprentice so that the best can be pulled out of them. If they cannot be humble enough to say, "Show me…. Teach me…. Guide me…," they will not make it to where they need to go.

We've covered a lot of ground and talked about four of the nine areas to groom for success. I established some great revelation in the very beginning, as far as the programming that happens to our kids: *expose, involve, and advance.* We talked about *influences* and the importance of that. We talked about *protection and control*. We talked about *spiritually equipping* children and several points on *people skills*. And last, we talked about *correction and accountability*.

I know you are starting to get the picture about what it really takes for your kids to become successful. I have a question for you at this point. How much have you already applied? Are you seeing any positive fruit yet? I am sure you are if you are doing any one of these strategies. Get ready because the next five are going to be really fun.

CHAPTER 9

STRATEGY #5: PREVENTION

A prudent man sees danger and takes refuge, but the simple keep going and suffer for it.

—**PROVERBS 22:3**

PREPARE YOUR KIDS IN ADVANCE!

It's important to talk to your kids about situations and behaviors before they are faced with them. This is called "Prevention" or "Preparation in Advance." *All* children want to succeed, and *all* children want to please their parents! When you prepare them in advance, you are setting them up for success instead of failure.

1. Public Setting and Conduct

If you take your kids into a public setting, like a restaurant, without preparing them, then anything goes and anything happens— there it is. They're wild, crazy, and spilling things. They are out of control, right? Well, guess what? You clearly deserved it because you didn't prevent those mistakes. You provoked those mistakes by not

185

girding them up ahead of time. To prevent this from happening, this is what I do:

Huddle Up/Pre-Game Talk to Your Kid(s)

When you talk to your children, it's important for you to smile. It says that you love them and that you know that they can succeed at what you are about to talk to them about. Then prepare and immunize them by telling them what they are about to experience. This pre-game talk is all about your guidelines. If you don't prepare them ahead of time, then you get what you get. Kids love structure; they can succeed in structure, it doesn't matter what the age. Let them know in advance where they are going and what they will be expected to do.

For example:

I'm taking our kids to a restaurant. As we're strapping our seat belts, I set them up in this manner:

"OK, guys, where are we going?"

"To a restaurant," they answer.

"Can you tell me the environment in a restaurant? Who's there? Are there big people or little people?"

"Mostly big people!"

"OK, and what kind of conduct are you to have?"

"We need to be quiet. We need to use inside voices. We need to have good manners. We need to be patient, and we need not to whine or complain."

"Awesome job! I'm so proud of you. We're going to have a great time. Now if you don't obey, there will be consequences, and you'll be disciplined for *deliberate disobedience.* That will take place in the bathroom of the restaurant or in the truck. I'm confident you can follow directions, obey, and set a good example for others to follow as you have done in the past. Are you guys ready? Can you do it?"

"Yes!"

"Awesome! OK. Let's go." And guess what? They're doing exactly what they have been asked to do.

When dinner is over, when our kids were good, I make a big deal out of it. I thank them sincerely and point out what each one did right and tell them how impressed I was. If they've messed up, I give a quick reminder of the talk we had in the vehicle.

I remember once at a Chinese restaurant in a real upscale, ritzy area, we brought our 1 and 3-year-old. Ordinarily that's a disaster waiting to happen, right? But afterward, two tables of diners came to compliment our kids. "When we saw you come in, we thought our dinner was going to be disturbed. We're so impressed. You have the most awesome kids we've ever seen."

Why did we get those compliments? I prepared our children before we went in on what to expect: what we expected, what the environment expected, and how they were to act. They were only 1 and 3. (This is exactly what I teach in the business world. It's called "A Call to Action" and "Prevention.")

Do you see how important it is to communicate with your children before an event? Your children really do want to please you, and if you prepare and motivate them beforehand, they will step up to the plate and do the right thing. Preparing our children how to respond properly in their environment teaches them how to honor us, themselves, and those who share the environment with them. This sets them up for success.

Five-Minute Warning

Let's say you're at a friend's house. All the kids are having fun, but it's time to leave. Should you go in and say, "All right, time to go!" NO! That's the wrong thing to do. You'll provoke resistance, complaining, and whining; besides, that's a cruel thing to do to them. If you want to receive honor, you must give it, remember? So instead, this is what I do.

Examples:

I want to honor our kids, so I'll tell them about the five-minute warning before we go to my friend's house. This prevents objections from them.

"OK, guys. Here's the deal. When I say, 'Hey, this is a five-minute warning. It's time to get everything cleaned up.' what should you say?"

"Yes, Mommy."

"With what kind of an attitude?"

"A good one," they answer.

"Awesome job! You guys are going to do great and set an awesome example."

And then we go.

When it's time to leave, I go in five minutes before and say, "Hey, guys, this is the five-minute warning. In five minutes, it's time to clean up and go home."

"Yes, Mommy."

"Awesome job—great response! I love the way you just responded to me. Great attitude! See you in five minutes."

Remember to always commend them when they've done a great job. How does this set them up for their future? They're learning to:

1. Honor.

2. Take an account of their environment.

3. Respond properly.

Prepare for the Babysitter

This is what I will say to our kids in front of the babysitter in order to prepare them. This way everyone is clear and everyone knows what's going on.

"OK, guys. Katie is going to be watching you tonight, and when she says it's time to clean your room or time for dinner, what will you say?"

"Yes, Katie."

"So, you won't say, 'Oh man, we don't want to.'"

"NO!"

"Awesome. When she says it is five minutes before bedtime, what will you say?"

"Yes, Katie."

This whole routine informs our children ahead of time what to expect, and it honors them. I'm also teaching them the proper way to honorably respond to the babysitter. They quickly realize that the rules haven't changed just because Mom and Dad are absent. This way everyone is on the same page: the babysitter, the kids, and us.

How does this set them up for their future? They are being trained to look ahead, make decisions, and plan their time wisely. When we're in the truck or car, I give our kids the plan on how to respond in the next situation. That is grooming them to successfully plan for their future.

Can you imagine if the people in your company knew the proper way to respond instead of flying off the handle and saying something stupid or walking away because of an ego trip? Imagine if you were groomed in this fashion. Imagine how much more successful your life would be if you knew to look ahead at what you're about to walk into instead of blindly walking into a scene and reacting inappropriately.

2. Environmental Check

Frame their minds and remind them constantly how they should be acting when going into any situation. Ask them what kind of environment they are entering and ask them about their surroundings. Remind them to honor their environment and the people around them by not screaming or yelling.

3. Post-Game Talk

This talk is just as important as the pre-game huddle. This is when you turn to them and celebrate their success; "You guys did great! Thank you for following directions." I verbally reward what I want to see more of and tell them that they did amazing and that they honored me by following directions. Then I remark on their individual achievements and efforts. I remind them that there is success in following directions. Their excitement level goes through the roof and they get excited about the next opportunity to be in a public setting with the family. Then when the next opportunity comes, they're ready to succeed again and be on their best behavior.

Kids love structure and they really want to please you. They succeed with structure. So if you don't give it to them, you get what you get. Then, instead of grooming them for success, you're grooming them for failure, now and in their future.

4. Teach Your Baby Sign Language

This is revolutionary! I shared with you earlier about a program called "preparation for parenting." This was my introduction to this revolutionary concept that really works.

Your babies can honor you and also stop being demanding or whiney. When you allow them to whine, then you've taught them it is OK to whine. But a baby who is 6 to 9 months old can be taught to communicate with you through sign language. It's amazing that they can understand you and you can know what they're thinking. Teaching them sign language prevents demanding and whining from babies. Let's face it, the only way they know how to naturally communicate is to scream or squirm. If you don't want them to whine or be demanding, then teach them to honor you.

Babies can communicate things like:

- **More!** Cup both of your hands facing each other with all of your fingers touching. Then tap them together. Do it with your baby's hands first and say "more" at the same time. They will understand this movement if you keep rehearsing it with them.

- **Please.** Make a circular movement in front of your belly. (This looks like you are rubbing it.) Show your baby how to do this. They'll learn that this is acting appropriately when they want something instead of being demanding.

- **I'm all done.** You'll know when they are done eating because they'll begin to start throwing things on the floor. Stop them instantly and grab their hands. Ask, "All done?" Then wave both of their hands in the air as the signal to say, "I'm all done."

- **Thank you.** After I've given them something like food or toys, I put one of their hands open under their mouth and make a forward gesture. It looks like urging someone to vomit.

- **No Whining!** Give the signal for "quiet and obey." I use this sign language and they learn what it means immediately. Look them in the eyes and quickly whisper, "Shoo," at the same time as you close one hand bringing all the fingertips together. Then slightly shake your head in a "no" gesture. Do this every time your child begins to whine. It really works.

These are the only signals I taught my babies because there's not too much else that they really want at that age. But it's still astounding to me that a little, tiny baby just barely past the vegetable stage can tell you exactly what they're thinking and wanting. Our last two kids taught me this; and these two have never whined or been demanding toward me. They've honored me, and it's been revolutionary. Why didn't I know this with the first three? Duh?

(View the video "Grooming the Next Generation for Success" to see the exact hand signals.)

5. Prevent Failure in School

Prepare your children to be successful in school with their teachers and classmates. Grades are important, but we're not raising performance-based or performance-accepted children. But we do want them to learn good people skills as soon as possible.

To do this, have a parent/teacher conference. Meet with their teachers and equip them on how to motivate your son or daughter. Explain the personality of your child and how to get the most out of them. Teach the teacher how to use your children as a leader in the class. I've done this with all our children and the teachers appreciate it. They call me up later to thank me and say how they enjoy better cooperation in their classroom as a result. This helps our son or daughter succeed, too, which is another way of grooming them for success.

Another great way to prepare and prevent failure in school is to not overload them with pressure. There's a high society idea of overloading kids with pressure for excellence. "You've got to get straight A's. You've got to be the best athlete. You've got to be the best piano player." (That is a high-strung workaholic parent placing their desires on their kid.)

I'm totally, 100 percent opposed to this attitude. If the child has the same personality as the parent and you're trying to pull the best out of him, then he needs to grow up learning and understanding that in life there will be some wins and there will be some losses. If in those losses he doesn't have a great attitude or sportsmanship skills, this will cause a problem, and he may not have another opportunity to play or to win. I teach our children not to change their attitude whether they win or not. *It is never the circumstances that determine success in life; it is how we deal with those circumstances that determine success.* I tell this to every crowd and to our children.

So again, do not overpressure your children to be performance-based and performance-accepted children. If they think they have to perform in order to be accepted by you, they'll grow up to be workaholics or the extreme opposite, lazy and non-productive, depending on their personality. (I've seen this. I've counseled many people about this problem.) They will grow up feeling that their worth and value is based on what they produce, that they're only loved for what they do, and that who they are isn't good enough.

People who are workaholics often have a very low self-worth. They feel like they have to perform in order to gain acceptance. They overcompensate for it with an egotistical arrogance and operate in fear-based control.

This is not healthy. Please don't overload your children. There has to be grace in the home.

6. Sex

This is a very important conversation to have with your kids at age 11. Unfortunately, by that age, they've perhaps already been exposed. *Passport to Purity* is a great tool to use, though. (You can purchase at Amazon.com or Christianbook.com)

The question is: will you allow or disallow programming, especially concerning the topic of sex, by television? If you allow the programming, then watch television with them so you can control its effect.

I discussed earlier that we live in a culture that promotes sex out of marriage. Since that's the case, there's a large list of consequences that kids are being subjected to and paying for simply by being programmed by television, conversations with friends, and the lack of parental guidance. Our kids are suffering big time, and many abortions have occurred as a direct result.

What am I grooming into our kids and all others I come in contact with, including yours depending on what you decide to do with this book? I am grooming that they will be virgins until marriage. I'm an active advocate for abstinence in order to prevent diseases, babies out of wedlock, and limited choices for their future, to name a few. There's no question that getting pregnant at age 14 limits one's choices for the future.

Virginity is so important to God, and I believe it is for our protection and for our blessing. However, virginity doesn't mean much to most people these days and this is sad. Very few people care about remaining pure prior to marriage. Everything goes and everything is accepted, including illicit sex. Right now, fifth graders are being taught in class how to put condoms on a banana and seventh graders are becoming pregnant. Why is this happening? It's because our children are being taught to have sex out of marriage.

Sex out of marriage leads to sex out of marriage, and that's the bottom line. The unfortunate thing is that most parents think that their kids know better no matter what the influences are. This also makes me very sad. The marriage bed was designed for virgins; there is an entire level of spiritual, physical, mental, emotional, and protection blessings they receive when they wait.

What I've personally witnessed from the kids who have saved themselves for marriage is a blessing from God that others who don't wait won't receive. The ones who wait don't walk into their marital relationship with a level of fear, insecurity, baggage, and open doors that those who have already had sex do. Instead, their relationship starts sanctioned, approved, and blessed by God with a higher level of trust, respect, honor, and fewer issues of deep-rooted, low self-worth feelings.

I've seen more troubles with couples in the first years of marriage who weren't virgins than those who were.

I've told my story hundreds of time. I have a past. I was not pure. Both of our daughters know that I was not married when they came into the world. At that time, I had hatred toward men, and I was going to hurt them all. That was my deal. This is why I'm grooming all of our children to be virgins when they marry. Otherwise, more problems are created that have to be cleaned up. Besides, I would like to give our kids the best possible chance for the best possible outcome.

Hans and I lived together for two years before we married and even had a child before marriage. But as soon as we married, everything changed negatively. Here's why. As soon as we exchanged vows, I hated him and I placed an unrealistic expectation on him to be something that he wasn't. I wanted him to protect, provide, lead, and be a spiritual head immediately after marriage—and he was none of those things at the time.

Before marriage, I didn't even think about these issues, consciously or unconsciously, and they didn't even matter to me on the day of the marriage. For the two years that we lived together before marriage, I had zero expectations of him. But after the marriage ceremony, I thought, *this is not the man I'm supposed to be married to.*

Something spiritual happened at the moment we exchanged vows. At that moment, we entered into a marriage covenant with God, and I instantly became a spiritual wife, and he, a spiritual husband. But that was not so when we were simply living together—we weren't husband or wife.

Sex is a spiritual thing; it's a covenant. Marriage is a covenant with God. Our culture has it backward and has really messed up what love is really about. In cultures that have arranged marriages, those marriages don't typically end in divorce and can last 40 or more years. In fact I heard recently from a client who was born and raised in Israel and was in an arranged marriage. She shared with me that the divorce rate is 2 percent. I believe it's because the original premise of marriage is biblically based and spiritually arranged by God. Parents prayed and chose the right suitor based on many important factors, such as purity of bloodline, culture, religion, finances, health, etc. Couples were matched to ensure the preservation of the bloodline, the wealth of the family, and the worship of their God.

"Don't marry those Canaanite women because they will bring in foreign gods." Too bad Solomon didn't take heed to this advice because this was his downfall. He married many foreign women, and each one brought her own foreign gods with her. When he began worshiping those gods, absolute destruction came upon him and his household for many generations.

Whenever I'm around a group of teens, I always discuss this matter because our culture has messed this up so much. My discussion goes something like this: "It's so interesting that we live in a culture that has sex and marriage completely backward. It's so backward that it has resulted in high divorce and abortion rates.

"But God has chosen a mate for you based on your parents' approval. This is Scriptural. No way did a daughter elope with someone who didn't meet her parents' approval. The parents were completely involved with the entire process of choosing the suitor. The match was based on financial, spiritual, and child-rearing purposes to ensure that their spiritual legacy would pass down to the *next generation*. If the marriage was to a foreigner, the parents couldn't guarantee that this would happen.

"In Bible days, couples didn't marry for *love*. Love had nothing to do with marriage; therefore it wasn't mandatory for the marriage arrangement. In fact, the marriage blessing spoken over the couple was that they would fall in love. But the marriage arrangement was strictly based on bloodline, children, financial blessings, and spiritual union with God. The girls were groomed to honor, respect, and serve their husbands and to bear children for the continuation of the family lineage.

"Today, couples marry for *love*. But their kind of *love* (lust or infatuation) is just a temporary emotion, especially if they've had sex out of marriage. That *love* is actually lust, seduction, and infatuation. These are the controlling emotions because as soon as it wears off, so does the desire to stay married. Resentment, bitterness, hatred, malice, and anger begin to chip away at the marriage over time, replacing the amorous feelings. Now the spouse makes them angry all the time. Day after day after day of this and the resentment becomes bigger than the love (lust or infatuation). This is when the couple says, 'we fell out of love,' after two, five, twenty years down the road, or after the children leave the nest.

"But I say, 'You weren't in love because you don't fall out of love, but you will fall out of lust, seduction, and infatuation.' So, be careful of our culture that says it's important to 'fall in love.' The majority of people in our culture, after a couple of years of marriage, will fall out of love. That's just how it works."

Then I challenge kids with this question, "Will you bring yourself to your marriage covenant pure or blemished? One comes with blessings beyond anything you could ever imagine; the other comes with consequences that you don't ever want to deal with."

I believe that our teenagers need to know the truth about love and marriage and that they should be groomed in this area as well.

7. *Know Their Personality*

If you're like most people, you've taken a personality quiz at one time or other. I took one about 20 years ago. It was then that I figured out that there were four different personalities, but I didn't have a clue how to communicate with them, identify them, or discover their individual characteristics. Plus, I needed a thesaurus in order to understand the words that were used to describe these different personalities.

After taking that test, I didn't let the learning end there. I began to study and watch people. I saw how they interacted, communicated, dressed, made decisions, and choose their occupations. I also observed their interests, weaknesses, and strengths. For the past 20 years, this is how I've learned about people, their motivations, and what makes them tick. I've taught what I've discovered in my business and personal development seminars for the past 18 years. But when it came time to begin teaching this lesson, I didn't feel confident calling these personalities by the terms others used like melancholy, choleric, sanguine, phlegmatic, colors, animals, or type ABCD.

I had a deep revelation about each personality and the similarities to beautiful gemstones and realized that gems start off in a raw form unrefined and very unpleasant. They are found in rock originally, but in the hands of a refiner, a stone becomes a gem of beauty. Gems are cut, chiseled, and placed under insane, intense heat in order to be set. These gems, including pearls, must go through a refinement process before they are complete, displayed, and sold.

Pearls are not found within rock but are created when a grain of sand embeds itself within an oyster shell. In order to get rid of the sand, the oyster will rub and rub, creating friction. This action is what creates a pearl, and the cost for one pearl can be in the thousands, especially the Tahitian black pearl (my personal favorite).

Just as gemstones, people start off in life in their raw form needing much refinement. Through the refining process, greater value is established. This is why I chose "gems" as identification titles for each one of the four personalities. Each personality has a name of a gem identifying its strengths, weaknesses, assets, and liabilities. We've found that people would much rather be called something of great value than something as ambiguous as a color, or something that's valueless. Gems are uplifting and very valuable.

We've shared the teaching of personality gems all over the world, and people easily use it in describing themselves and their children.

We stress the importance of identifying the primary gem, as well as the secondary gem in their children, and using the information to groom them.

Everyone has a portion of each gem within them and also the ability to refine these secondary gems that may be lying dormant in them. If they do, they will be creating a well-rounded person who has accessed the strengths of each personality and refined the weaknesses in their own personality. Since there are inherent strengths and weaknesses in every single gem, when children are identified early on, the parent can totally refine those weaknesses so that they don't become a terrible disaster for them in the future. I've seen this in adults, I've seen it in myself, and I've tested it while grooming my children.

By knowing your child's dominant and secondary gems, you'll know how to communicate with and motivate them. You'll know what they are really lacking and how to strengthen them in that particular area or gem.

As I discuss gems, I will refer to our kids as examples to illustrate the four personalities: Sapphire, Pearl, Emerald, and Ruby. Our children have been groomed in the various gems. Some are very dominant and others are well-rounded like our daughter, Arika.

Sapphire Personality

This is the child to whom you often have to say, "Don't cross that line," and they put their toes on the line—argh!

Strengths

A Sapphire is verbal and loud. They're fun. They're wild. They love loud music. A Sapphire talks constantly. They even talk in their sleep. The minute they get out of bed, they're talking, and they're constantly telling stories. There's no pause in their communications. I mean, they just go on and on and on and on and on.

They're usually not orderly, but they are very visionary. These are the kids who continuously wear their shoes on the wrong feet and their clothes inside out and backwards. They're very encouraging and are natural motivators. In fact, they thrive on encouragement. They are pot-stirrers who love to laugh, and their laugh is infectious. Everything has to be fun. They are major multitaskers and big-time risk-takers. These are the ones who are going to jump off the bunk bed to see how far they can jump. These are the ones who end up with broken legs and arms. They like to have fun clothes and lots of accessories. They love changing their hair often and making it as wild as it can be. When the boys are young, they don't mind having a cool bedhead, oh and they often forget to bring their lunch even though they just packed it. They also can make toys out of trash, buildings for their GI Joe's out of a box or styrofoam.

If you want to motivate them to do something, use teamwork because they love teamwork and they love people. They love popularity, excitement, and parties. They love all that kind of stuff, and when you know this about your child, then you'll know how to motivate them to follow your instructions.

Roman, at 9 months, entertained the entire family at the dinner table even though he could still be classified as being in the semi-vegetable stage. At the time, Hans' brother, our nanny (who is our sister-in-law now), Hans, me, 5-year-old Arika, and 3-year-old Cabe would be entertained by his antics. The whole table of kids and adults would laugh, completely under Roman's control. Roman would make Cabe laugh with funny faces and noises. Then we would laugh because Cabe would turn blue from laughing so hard. Every night to this day, this now 11-year-old continues to entertain everyone.

You will know a Sapphire at birth. Roman came out screaming and didn't stop until turning nine. (We've had two years without him screaming. Hallelujah!) All our kids listen to music all night long. When I go upstairs after they've gone to sleep, Roman's lights are still on; his wild worship music is playing loudly while he sleeps.

Weaknesses

The Sapphire's weakness is focusing. They have a hard time with this, and they're usually the daydreamers in the classroom. They are the ones usually talking and distracting everybody else in the room because their brains are hyperactive. Their schoolwork is totally out of order and very messy; disorganized and late.

Everything is random for them because that's just the way they think. In fact, when they do their math homework, they'll skip problems 1-5 and go to number 6, then down to number 17 before going up to number 14, and then number 1.

The sad thing about this group is that most people don't know how to motivate them and consequently ridicule them. In school, they are the ones who get in the most trouble and are often in the principal's office. They are also the ones on Ritalin (a drug given to ADD or ADHD kids). This is very sad and extremely unfortunate because they are very creative, and the medication kills their creativity.

Sapphires overreact when things don't go right, and their feelings get hurt very easily. They are often tempted to take offense, which will destroy their lives. Their lives are all about people, so if they take offense, the offense becomes poison and eats and rots their soul. For a Sapphire, offense opens the door to distrust, blame, hatred, malice, resentment, bitterness, and unforgiveness.

A Sapphire wears their emotions. You can see it all over their faces and know exactly what's going on in them. Others would label this as bi-polar because of the extreme emotional highs and lows. So happy and then so sad; but they won't stay in sadness for long, depending on their childhood and past.

Roman can be so joyful one second, and in another moment, as sad as all get out, based on what somebody said to him. I constantly have to tell him, "Say no to offense." Or, "Roman, what should you say no to?"

He'll answer, "Offense."

"That's right, and what should you say yes to?"

"Joy"

It's a conscious decision that he has to make.

Grooming—Groom their weaknesses without condemning them.

Unfortunately, most people don't know how to motivate a Sapphire. Because they have a strong leadership gifting and are very extreme, loud, bold, and boisterous in their personality, they can be groomed to lead the classroom to do their work. They love to help, they love recognition, and they love reward.

Sapphires love people and often have the most friends out of all the gems. In fact, when they become adults they are the gem who is still in contact with most of their school friends, even the ones from kindergarten. They love to use their gifts of boldness and enthusiasm, so you absolutely want to groom that heart to overcome their weaknesses by using their strengths.

The spiritual gifts are talked about in the Bible, and as I've studied the Bible and people, I have found that each gem has spiritual gifts as well. You can find the topic of spiritual gifts in First Corinthians 12 and Romans 12. The spiritual gifts of a Sapphire are to motivate and to encourage. Use those gifts in your classrooms and in your household. Get them to motivate everybody else. It's just gorgeous. A Sapphire wants to be recognized by you and doesn't want to disappoint you. They can sink into a deep depression if they feel like they're failing. Not good. Here comes rebellion and retaliation big time.

First, start with encouragement. If you start with an encouraging word for a Sapphire, you can get them to do anything. Teachers can use this strategy at school.

"Roman, you're always so good at motivating the class. I love your excitement and the way you love teamwork. So can you help me out? We have to get this work (homework, housecleaning, or other chores) done in about 20 minutes. You're so good at helping everybody. Can you help me to get everyone to do it in less time, say 15 minutes, then we can take an early recess?"

"OK!" He'll be the first one to get excited and enthusiastic and ready to follow the plan. He'll also pull that vision, "Come on, guys. We can do it!" Unfortunately, most teachers don't know how to motivate a Sapphire and they end up butting heads with them because they feel like they're out of control.

For Example

Kids can be motivated to do anything. Since Sapphires typically are unorganized, their bedrooms are disasters. But that's not the case with our son, Roman. In fact, I've been grooming his heart to appreciate order.

"Order helps save time so you can go have as much fun as you want later!" Rather than, "Clean your room because I said so! Clean it, or else!" That isn't going to work with a Sapphire, but this will. "Hey, dude, check it out. You know how you want to go swimming?"

"Yes!"

"OK, look, right now we have to do this task in your room. We have to get your toys and your drawers organized and make sure that we're ready to go because if God can trust us with keeping these things in order, then He's going to bless us with all kinds of fun. OK, so how much time do you think it will take?"

"15 minutes."

"Do you want me to time you?"

"Yes."

"Ready? On your mark, get set, go!" That's what you do with a Sapphire. I'm not kidding you; a timer with a Sapphire is amazing. They have fun working, and then they come out, "I did it!" High-five and "Oh, you're so awesome!" They love it.

"Roman, hey buddy would you be willing to help me with some teamwork? I love the way you are such a team player. Let's get everybody excited about getting all this done so we can go to the lake early." These are the things that get them excited.

Pearl Personality

This is the child who stays far from the line and obeys the first time.

Strengths

Pearls naturally have a heart to fulfill the needs of people. They listen well and love people. They love to help. They love to serve. They love to love. In the home, they naturally want to help with dishes and with laundry. It's absolutely incredible. They're warm, very sensitive, calm and even-keeled. They're compliant, honest, loyal, mellow and quiet. They don't butt their heads up against authority and don't like confrontation. So they'll do anything to keep the peace because they want everyone to be happy.

They are most comfortable alone or in small group settings of 1-3 people maximum, and they love the arts. They're very musical and love to worship. Pearls love to show mercy; that's their spiritual gifting. They feel for that hurt puppy. When they get older, they feel for the homeless. They feel for the whales—things like that. Their spiritual gifts are to heal, to intercede, to show mercy, and to serve. They typically like to wear clothes that are comfortable and more earthy colors or something special that was given to them. They enjoy hand-me-downs because it is sentimental when given to them by someone they love (which is almost anyone). They like to be outside and hike, search for living creatures, play in the dirt, and explore. They like to build houses for bugs or butterflies, and they like to talk to them too. They are the easiest kids to raise because they are typically quiet and compliant. And they are very touchy feely. They love hugs and snuggles.

Our daughter Arika is very well-rounded in all of the gems. She has a strong Pearl side to her, as well as a Sapphire and Ruby. An Emerald had to be groomed into her because it didn't come naturally.

They are very creative as well. They like to paint, crochet, sew, play music, and so forth.

We put an acoustic guitar in our daughter's hand when she was 14, and it was as if she'd been playing for three or four years. In fact, Isa, who is a professional, couldn't believe it. At a birthday party, she got out the guitar and she's strumming and singing at the same time with Isa.

"Is this your first time?" asked Isa.

"Yes," Arika answered. It was just a natural gift.

Weaknesses

If the Pearl heart is not groomed properly, they become people-pleasers and have co-dependent relationships. They also have a tendency of getting their feelings hurt very easily because they want everybody to be happy. They're sad when things don't go right with people.

Grooming

Pearls care a lot about what people think about them because they want to please everybody. They also have a tendency of easily being taken advantage of. It's important that you groom their hearts with boundaries and boldness. There is a gift of boldness in them. You just have to pull it out.

I know that Pearls have it in them because I've watched Pearls get very passionate about different 'causes' they are supporting. I've seen Pearls be very bold. You will have to absolutely groom boldness in them and help them set boundaries so that they won't be taken advantage of.

Emerald Personality

This is the child who stays a few inches from the line.

Strengths

An Emerald is one who pays attention to details, facts, and figures. They have the ability to simplify complicated things and the ability to solve a lot of problems all at once. They see solutions in ways that other people cannot see them. They like lists and making plans. They love puzzles and solving problems because they are extreme thinkers—they think a lot. And once they learn something, you don't have to remind them again.

They're very predictable and very similar to a Pearl in their disposition in that they are more quiet, compliant, and like to be alone. However they are not people-pleasers and are very comfortable being themselves. They like to be who they are, and they are very confident. They often see what's wrong in a situation and have no problem pointing it out. They're not as wild and bold as a Ruby or a Sapphire, but can be very direct.

These are the kids who like to wear their clothes perfectly, with no spots, no wrinkles. The boys button their shirts all the way to the top, tuck them in, and want a belt. They like to look nice. They are very conscientious about their hair being in the right place and are never bedheads.

They naturally want to keep things clean. They like schedules and routines. Whatever the routines are, they do it automatically. (For example, cleaning the kitchen after dinner—they automatically step into the routine.) They can't stand it when a routine is changed.

The Emerald is orderly and timely, never late. They also have a spiritual gift of teaching, discernment, and wisdom. They have a heart for righteousness, with a clear sense of what's right and wrong.

Emeralds avoid large groups; they'd rather be alone. They like to entertain themselves and will do homework by themselves, rarely asking for help, even in kindergarten. In fact, our son Micah would receive his week's homework package and do it all on the first day.

Micah is very matter-of-fact, detail-oriented, and orderly. When he was 2 years old he kept his room spotless. I didn't even have to tell him or teach him how to do it. He just got out of bed and made it. He'd take off his clothes and put them in the laundry. He still does it. Why? It's order. That's an Emerald. A Sapphire takes off their clothes and they land on the floor.

Micah likes to be alone. He can play in all the chaos, but he also will withdraw and read a book by himself or play with Legos. As a 1-year-old, we would find him in the corner trying to button his shirt for a solid 30 minutes. Emeralds are very persistent. He would also take our belts and loop them together for hours at a time. Now he has moments of wildness and then moments of being very quiet and very subdued. He's a thinker. Emeralds think a lot and they have an amazing, amazing authority that they've been born with.

Weaknesses

Emeralds are perfectionists and they want to have all their ducks in a row before they make a move. Micah would line up his vitamins on the table in a row then take them one at a time. Cabe, our Ruby, would swallow four at a time. It often takes an emerald longer to finish something. Emerald adults actually have a hard time getting started because they take so much time in preparation because they want everything to be perfect. They are not spontaneous risk-takers like a Sapphire, who says, "OK, lets go!" at the drop of a hat. When things don't go right, they complain or actually can really rail someone for their incompetency and with their authoritative and interrogative manner it often puts people on the defense and doesn't accomplish much. A Ruby also will use their authority to prove that you're wrong and stupid and he's right, and a Ruby will argue just for the sake of arguing. An Emerald will argue because they are actually right, always right, and they will tell you that.

Grooming

I have to tell you this one little story about Micah when he was 4. We were in Los Angeles in a hotel and just getting back from Disneyland with my handicapped mother who uses a walker. We were standing in the elevator and waiting for Mom to enter when a man who was at the control panel pushed the floor button and closed the door on my mom.

Micah left my side, went over to the man, pointed and glared at him and said, "You're not supposed to do that. You were supposed to wait for my Grandma." Then he turned around and came back to Hans and me.

The man responded, "Oh, I'm sorry."

You see, Emeralds are born with this authority. It's amazing! An Emerald comes out with it. If you're wrong, you're wrong. That's the way it is. So obviously, we needed to correct Micah and teach him better people skills. We had to teach him, "You need to honor and respect your elders." I thought, *Does he know he's only two feet tall? Does he have any idea how little he is?*

No, he didn't have an idea at all about how small he was. It's incredible how he saw something was wrong and then called it out. That was probably not the best way to get someone to realize that he was wrong, but Micah totally convicted that man.

"Micah, you need to honor and respect your elders!"

"Oh, OK."

"Now, apologize to that man."

"I'm sorry, sir. Please forgive me for not honoring you."

Throughout my experience with working with Emeralds, people skills is one of their biggest weakness. They are often judged as being cold hearted and insensitive. They also need to have humility groomed into them. Because of them being so "perfect" in their own eyes and often seeing how imperfect everyone else is, they do have an issue of pride. Thirdly because of this perfectionist attitude as I stated earlier, they often don't get started or take a long time to get started. To combat this, I teach Emeralds to shift the goal to this philosophy, "It's not about perfection; its about getting the job done with results." I then tell them to test the results and improve from there. This saves a massive amount of time and has helped my Emerald clients become far more productive

Ruby Personality

This is the child who often crosses the line or wants to take charge and move it.

Strengths

Rubies always seem to have to be the head of everything. Since they have to be the best at everything, they don't surround themselves with other people who are better than they are. That is one of the biggest struggles I've seen in people in charge of companies; they don't surround themselves with people who are better than they are.

They are leaders who have to dominate. They have to be the best. They have to win. They're warriors. They're strong. They're passionate. They're driven. They have strong desires. They like to be in authority and take charge. They're very determined and naturally confident and bold. They're also natural goal-setters.

He or she could be a dominant leader who leads by fear: "It's my way or the highway!" He or she could also be an equipper who leads people into freedom—to believe and to go for it, to move out in their gifting and their calling. Rubies are amazing, and their spiritual gifting is in leadership and governing.

These are the kids who want all the best clothes, shoes, and stuff. They really care about having name brands and what is popular. They strive to be the best at everything they do, sports, school, games, and so forth. In fact if they can't win, they won't play, and say the game is "stupid."

Weaknesses

Rubies are bossy and dominating. They get angry when things don't go right. They can be manipulative and pushy and perceived as arrogant and cocky. They will go through ruts in their lives and eventually suffer from severe depression if they are not groomed right. They may also go through some major highs and lows and even get themselves into a destructive pattern. The vast majority of Rubies I have interviewed or worked with suffer from burn-out, which leads to depression.

They have a tendency to be unteachable. "I know. I know. I know how to do that." They are self-reliant and independent.

"No, the answer is, 'Yes, Mom. I agree with you,' instead of, 'Oh, I know.'

You really have to watch ego and arrogance with a Ruby. Those are major weaknesses and a road they typically go down. You know what happens to egotistical, arrogant people—they don't stay married long. In business, they try and fail often. Some of them can continue a business, but they're miserable. They have no friendships, so they hire people to be their friends. That's no joke!

Grooming

If you don't groom your Ruby child's heart in the right way, they'll be dictators controlling by fear. They will not have a healthy marriage or career. However, if you do groom them, they'll become amazing leaders and lead well in every area of their lives.

Here's what it is. Rubies are extremely overconfident so you have to reach their heart. You have to teach them how to be teachable. That's how I'm grooming this son of mine who's a Ruby and totally geared toward the best, having to be first, and having to win.

You have to look at those possible weaknesses for the future and try to groom their hearts to be humble, to serve, to be honorable. Teach them to pull out the best in others instead of competing with them all of the time.

If your Ruby wants to be a professional athlete, teach him or her how to work with diligence now with the household chores. "If you can be trusted working with diligence, you'll diligently complete this project. If you can be diligent here, then being diligent later will be so easy for you."

Rubies show initiative and take charge. They're very determined, naturally confident, and bold. They have to be the best. They're big thinkers, and they're fast. They accomplish more then any other gem in shorter periods of time because they are doers and they do it now. They have a history-making, world-shaking mindset which means that they have to do something big and great with their lives.

Character has to be developed in them. Keep constantly reminding and helping them to continually make decisions toward their goals. For example, Cabe wants to lead people, whether it's his classroom with his teachers, kids who are older or younger, or his siblings at home.

So, we say, "OK, awesome! You know what? You have two younger brothers and an older sister. If you're going to lead, you'll need to know how to lead women and men and those younger and older than you are. So look at this, Cabe. Look at what a blessing this is for you right now."

Note

Most parents try to change their kids to be like themselves. For example, Emerald parents with a Sapphire child often fall into condemning their child for being disorganized instead of learning how to motivate the child to be organized. A Ruby parent often tries to get a bigger reaction out of their Pearl child or puts them down because they are not risk-takers.

Don't try to change your child. Learn how to motivate their strengths and train up their weaknesses without condemnation so their weaknesses are not inhibited in the future. Embrace the fullness of each gem in your home. They were designed that way for a reason. The truth is that we all need each other; an Emerald adult should recruit a Sapphire to plan a party. The Sapphire will do an amazing job quickly, and it will be a huge success. A Ruby should recruit a Pearl to help keep proper relationships with clients or employees. Each gem is significant in life's big picture.

My perception about gems is that God gave each of us a portion of who He is to demonstrate His strength, beauty, and every facet. Not any one person has it all. I also believe we are to learn to work together in unity instead of division. God's unity is not everyone conforming to what one man or woman thinks. Nothing in creation is exactly the same. We are all originals and unique in some away. Even identical twins are not exactly the same. Their DNA is different as are their fingerprints and the number of hairs on their heads. Our lack of wisdom tries to get man to conform to man. This is foolishness. God's unity is diversity in harmony. It is appreciating the strengths and weaknesses of each gem and then saying, "Hey, he is better at this than I am. I'll ask him to help me with this," and then, "What can I help him with?"

Go back and read this section again on gems, and you will see that each gem needs the other to be successful and to get the job accomplished holistically and beautifully. Working with each other would not be possible unless we recognized each others' strengths and weaknesses and appreciated our differences. For instance, don't place an expectation on Sapphires to be on time—they're always late. But you can definitely expect an Emerald to be on time. Don't expect a Ruby who has not been groomed correctly to be a servant. No, they'd rather be served. The servant quality has to be groomed in them. Rubies will have to be refined in order for selfishness to be rooted out of them. (God is the answer for refining all gems.) You can definitely expect a Pearl to desire to serve; but you can't expect them to want to win. They don't care about winning; they just want to help and serve.

CHAPTER 10

STRATEGY #6:
WORK VERSUS PLAY

Lazy hands make a man poor, but diligent hands bring wealth.

—**PROVERBS 10:4**

YOUR KIDS MUST VALUE WORK
FIRST, THEN PLAY!

Let me remind you that this is not a book about how to raise mediocre, apathetic, non-dreaming, average kids with no vision. This is a program on how to increase your children's odds for success. It will prepare them to be divinely placed in the marketplace and chosen for the better jobs and promotions or for success as entrepreneurs in the business world. This program is to train your children to have fruitful marriages and to be great parents raising great kids having a great life full of adventure.

A majority of the people in our nation and the world today has stopped learning and refuse to be coached or to invest in their personal development. There is a lot more to learn after you graduate from high school or college—and it's not always free.

We have to raise the *next generation* to be willing to learn from others who do what they want to do and are doing it well. Many people only have excuses for why they aren't successful. All they do to prove their point is argue and whine, murmur, and complain. They dig their heels in saying, "I'm right and everybody else is wrong."

They're broke, that's the bottom line. Ego and excuses will keep them broke for the rest of their lives. Excuses will keep us all broke if we are not careful. I'm passionate about this because many times I've watched adults who have everything it takes to make it and everything it takes to make a difference in their lives, and they don't do anything with it. Why? Because they were groomed that way.

I know the desire of my parents' heart was for me to succeed. I believe that is true for all parents; they just don't know how to make it happen. But after reading this book, you'll have enough information to know how to make this happen for your children.

1. *You have to paint a future picture for them.*

Our Ruby son is very driven, very dominant, and has strong leadership qualities. When he was first born (I had two girls first), I noticed a strong defiance in him that wasn't in our daughter, Arika, who's a Pearl. Arika was more compliant and submissive. But our son was like, "Whoa!"

God made boys to dominate. That's how He created them. He gave them dominion. He created Adam first, Eve second. He created them to take control, to dominate, to lead. That's the way they were made. I found myself, when he was two, wanting to squelch that leadership quality in him because I didn't know any better.

As a businesswoman coaching adults, I saw the hindrances and the pain in dominant men who were put down by dominant mothers.

These mothers didn't know how to nurture the heart of their sons or teach them how to lead properly when they were children. I saw the toil that was placed on these men. They were suffering, afraid of failure, and couldn't succeed because of how they were raised.

Mom and Dad, when it comes to work and play, this is the deal. Your sons were born to dominate. They were born to take dominion. That's natural, so don't squelch it. But definitely nurture it in the right direction.

Our son, Cabe, has a very dominant, take-charge kind of personality, but as his parent, *I'm* the one in charge. There was a bit of a conflict here. The main challenge I had with him was his work ethic. He's a strong athlete, but he doesn't want to help at home. Why? It didn't come natural to him to help; but it came natural for Arika, who had a lot of Pearl/Sapphire and loves to help. She would play the cooking game and pretend to be a housekeeper, doing this and that. She turned everything into a game of service, and she loved it.

But here comes this boy who doesn't want to help do anything and pitches a bad attitude when it's time clean his room or do any chore he didn't want to do. I had not experienced this before, and soon I had three sons—*ugh!* Anyway, this is how I handled the issue: *I had to paint a picture of his future.*

Here are two biblical guidelines concerning work ethics:

> *Lazy hands make a man poor, but diligent hands bring wealth* (Proverbs 10:4).

> *To one he gave five talents of money, to another two talents, and to another one talent, each according to his ability...* (Matthew 25:15-16).

God gives gifts according to ability, and we're the ones in control of the ability. We own our ability, can determine what that ability is, and can get blessed with more if we handle what we have. That's how it works. Read the rest of chapter 25 in Matthew.

I knew that if our son didn't *want* to help, it was a sign of him *not wanting to work*. He didn't like chores or anything other than what he wanted to do. Obviously, what he wanted to do was to play, win games, do sports-related stuff like wrestling with Dad. But when it came time to do the dishes, the bad attitude came in, and we'd have to say, "Hold on there, buddy."

I sat him down one day and told him, "Cabe, you know what? God made you a leader and has given you a strong leadership gift, and with that you're going to help lead others. I want to know, do you want to help them succeed or do you want to help them fail?"

"Succeed."

"We were put on this planet to work. That's what we were put on this planet to do, and you can do it with a spirit of excellence so that you'll be promoted to bigger and better things. But if you can't be trusted with a good attitude on these small things, then you're going to have to keep doing these small things for the rest of your life until you get it done right with a right attitude."

Unless you are faithful in small matters, you won't be faithful in large ones. If you cheat, even a little, you won't be honest with greater responsibilities. This is the basis of my work ethic.

So the questions are:

- Do I want my kids to hate work, or do I want them to enjoy it?

- Do I want them to do it with a spirit of excellence or a spirit of bitterness?

- Do I want them to do it with a spirit of gratefulness that they can serve and work, or do I want them

to do it with a spirit of ungratefulness that leads
to murmuring, arguing, and complaining?

Can you imagine if your parents taught you to enjoy work? Imagine if they taught you how to look at it in a totally different light—that it's a privilege to have the gift to work. Imagine if you, yourself, had a different attitude about the work that you do.

"Oh, man, I can't believe we have to do this. I hate doing this stuff. It's just such a joke. I wish I was doing other things."

Great attitude. Not! That attitude will never get you a promotion. Whether you know it or not, whether you believe in God or not, there's somebody watching. You may think it's your boss, and sometimes it might be, but the Creator of the heavens and earth is always taking notes. When you have a spirit of excellence and gratefulness and you look at your work as a privilege and as a stepping stone to greater things, a whole different line of fruit comes out of the work that you do. You'll be placed on an acceleration track and promoted quickly.

Because I knew this, it was important that our son be groomed in this area. I'd seen lazy sons of other parents who just wanted to play all the time. Everything was centered on them, and they turned into lazy men wasting time with video games and television. If your children want to play and party all the time and think the whole world is centered on them, that is not the formula for a good husband or father. It's certainly not a good formula for a 6 or 7-figure income-earning father. No way! It's not a formula to get promoted in your job or to build a good size business or successful ministry in the community, either. It's not a good formula for anything.

I knew that I had to find a way to motivate our son to change his attitude. His work ethic needed to be at least equal with play because if his attitude stunk with work, he wasn't going to *want* to do it. I needed to nurture his heart to enjoy the chores that he had and to *want* to do them. I knew it all rested on the presentation because children are moldable and pliable. They're jars of clay, and so are we for that matter.

Now, back to you. Imagine if you were taught not to cut corners. For example:

- You're in a grocery store going through the produce aisle; you grab a couple of grapes and eat them. *You're teaching your child how to steal.*

- When the phone rings and your kid answers the phone, and you say, "Tell him I'm not home," *you're teaching them how to lie.*

- When you gripe and murmur and complain about duties around the house, *you're teaching them how to hate their work.*

If our attitudes are not right about our work, we'll be like the children of Israel wandering in the wilderness for 40 years. Pardon me—but no, thank you! I don't want that for our son, and I don't want that for me. So it's important that you absolutely grab that heart and teach your son or daughter how to find the "good" in the work that they do. Teach them that it's a privilege and an honor, and most of all, that it's preparation for what's to come.

Cheat even a little, and you won't be honest with greater responsibilities. Therefore, you'll never get the greater responsibilities. If you can't be trusted with what you have now, you certainly won't get promoted to the next step. I groomed our son's heart to understand this while he was young. Now that he's older, it's easier for him.

In the beginning, when he was two and didn't want to clean his room, I made a game out of it. I found what he liked to do, and I did it with him and turned it into a sports game. (I didn't even know he was going to be an athlete. At the age of 2, you never really know.) He was actually 18 months old when he started to learn how to clean his room. So this is what I did. I had Arika, who was compliant and easy, and groomed to love to lead—come in and play with us.

I'd say, "Hey, Arika! Let's do this fun game. I'm going to be a sports announcer." I stood at one end of the bedroom and basically motivated Cabe to *want* to clean his room by announcing:

"Oh, man! There's Cabe Johnson. Look at him. He just picked up that Elmo giggly guy, and he—oh, wow! Look at how fast he's going over there to put Elmo in the toy box. And oh, look at Arika Johnson! Whoa, man! She's got a home run over there. Look at that. She just grabbed all those books at once and put them in the bookshelf. Whoa! There's Cabe Johnson again! Look at that. He's picking up that blanket. Boy, look at him fold that thing. That's just amazing!"

It took about a week of me doing this to the point when I could say, "Cabe, go clean your room." He'd get in there—boom, boom, boom—"I'm done!" Why?

I discovered, first of all, that he was a Ruby and loved to win and get things done. He likes working, now.

Teach your kids how to love their work. Find something that they can love about it. Encourage them whenever you see them doing what you're trying to groom in them to do. Here's another example about Cabe because he was our biggest challenge, although he is no longer.

"OK, Cabe, it's time to put away the dishes."

"Oh, man!"

"Do you want to try that again?" (I taught about this response earlier in the book.) "Cabe, this dishwasher is being used to groom your heart to someday lead other people. You want to succeed in life with leading other people, right? How do you want others to respond to you when you are asking them to do a task that needs to be done? However you respond to those leading you will determine how others will respond to you in the future as you are leading them."

Or,

"That washing machine is being used right now, Cabe, to begin to groom and refine you to be able to possibly lead a corporation someday. Your attitude of: 'I don't want to do that,' and 'this sucks' is not the attitude of someone who succeeds in life. The attitude of 'I don't want to' and 'I want to be lazy' is the attitude of somebody who winds up dependent on the government or in jail someday if you follow that road all the way out. They have no money, so they'll eventually have to steal it from somebody else. They'll take advantage of people. Cabe, do you want to do great things in your life?"

"Yes, Mom."

"Then that washing machine, that dishwasher, and that bedroom are things that are being used to refine your heart. So when the time comes and you've shown yourself to be responsible, you've shown yourself to have a good attitude with the things you're entrusted with right now, these small responsibilities that seem big to you are grooming you for great responsibilities in the future."

Our son now has a different attitude about work. He responds quickly with a spirit of excellence.

I began to shepherd his heart with this message and then afterward, I'd say, "Awesome job, Cabe! I'm proud of that attitude you had through that, man. Look at you! Smile on your face. You did it diligently. You did it quickly." I encouraged him on the things that would matter for the future—for a job or for a marriage. I decided early that I wasn't going to raise a man who wouldn't lift a finger in the house. Not an option.

I wasn't going to raise a man who couldn't take care of himself and would sit around saying, "Serve me." That was not the option here. That would not create a great, successful marriage later. That type of attitude actually causes pain in marriages, no question.

So my heart with our sons is that they'll know how to care for themselves and that they would be team players with their wives someday, raising their families together in a balanced way instead of a usury manner.

Usury stinks, my friends. It stinks. And if you're not raising your daughters to serve, to help, and to love it, then eventually she's going to use some man. This is where we see some men who serve in every capacity in the household. He does the laundry, the dishes, the cooking, and works all day long while she's online, partying, or having a cup of coffee with friends, etc. I've seen the fruit of this. I know what those pictures look like. Because of my years of counseling, I've seen what has destroyed marriages.

It all amounts to this, we are responsible for grooming our children's hearts to enjoy work so that we don't raise a bunch of lazy complainers looking for a cheap way out. When it comes to money and success, he *who chases fantasies ends in poverty.* We were put here to work, and it's our job to groom our children's hearts to want to work because quite naturally, they don't want to. Groom them with a right attitude toward work, and then encourage what's positive and in the right direction.

2. First comes responsibility, and then comes play.

There are many parents today trying hard to compete with someone else. They've been programmed that the more activities their kid is in (whether it's dance, piano, soccer, Tae Kwan Do, or gymnastics) the better it is. Their kids do all of this in a week, plus schoolwork and family life. But there is no family life if all of these things are going on.

I know about this lifestyle personally, and I have a lot of kids. We don't participate in a lot of activities for this reason: life is not centered on extracurricular activities. Life is centered on God and family. If an opportunity arises briefly for a sports activity or music lesson, then maybe we'll decide to participate. But our children understand that family comes first, not playing.

When it comes to play, many times I've seen mothers heading toward nervous breakdowns. Their children are involved in too many different activities and are overwhelmed with no idea of responsibility or accountability. The kids have to eat supper late at night because that's when they return home from this or that practice. The family doesn't have a meal together because Mom is trying to get kids to and from different activities. She's totally stressed out and so are the kids.

Here's the deal. Our son has to earn the right to play hockey. He has to earn the right to play basketball. He has to earn the right to play baseball and soccer. This is what I tell him:

"Cabe, if you can handle this chore with the right attitude and the same amount of excellence that you have on that hockey rink or the basketball court, if you can show that you're responsible right here with these things, then you'll be blessed to play hockey. And while you're playing hockey, this responsibility has to be upheld with the same level of excellence and attitude."

This is how he earns the right to be rewarded for doing what he loves to do and it now becomes the source of (a) motivation and (b) discipline.

"Cabe, if you don't take care of your room, then you're saying you don't want to play hockey. Do you understand?"

"Yes, Mom."

"So, if I come home and this isn't done, you're saying, 'I don't want to go to my hockey game,' right?"

"Yes."

"Do you want to go to your hockey game?"

"Yes!"

"Are you going to clean your room?"

"Absolutely!"

There you go—leverage. Work first, and then play. Children have to keep up with their responsibilities and with what they're entrusted with at home. This prepares them for success in the future. If they have zero responsibility and everything is centered on their activities, then they're being prepared for future failure.

Most kids are stressed out because they just can't do it all. Many kids in the United States are involved in many after-school extracurricular activities. I've seen kids with circles under their eyes and some of them hate the activities that they are being forced to participate in. But, "Oh, we're pushing them to be extraordinary adults." I'm sorry, but the piano, soccer, gymnastics, and this and that, aren't forming them to succeed. The bottom line: if you have an Olympic gymnast in your home without household responsibilities, when their career as an Olympic gymnast is over in their 20s, then what? Think about that. What kind of parents are they going to be? What kind of spouses will they be? There will be major issues and fights because they don't know how to clean their rooms, do their own laundry, or take care of the dishes. Work first, and then play.

3. Excellence, order, and a proper attitude about chores are mandatory!

You've seen kids and adults who don't have the spirit of excellence and don't realize that they should have it. There is carelessness about what they do and the wrong attitude regarding it. When things are in order, like drawers or the living room, stress is eliminated because you know exactly where everything is, which makes you feel better.

Let me tell you how this works. I have our little guy, Roman, who just loves this term. "I'd be glad to, Mom."

I'll say, "Hey, Roman, Mommy needs you to help me make dinner."

"I'd be glad to, Mom."

"Hey, Roman, can you please take out the trash."

"I'd be glad to, Mom."

"Roman, can you put the dishes away?"

"I'd be glad to, Mom."

"Roman, can you go upstairs and take a shower?"

"I'd be glad to, Mom." Why does he say that? Because he's been taught that "I'd be glad to" is the right response and attitude when asked to do something. So it's instant. If any of our children say this with a bad attitude, they know that they will be reprimanded because I instantly see if their body language and words add up.

When the response and attitude is proper, I make a big deal out of it. "Oh my gosh, Roman, I love your attitude and response. It's amazing and so honorable. It really blesses God and us when you truly honor your parents."

When teaching or grooming your children for excellence in the area of work, let's look at the example of Roman's battle with handwriting. I home schooled this one for a year, and his handwriting was out of control. He's a lefty, and his writing was all over the place.

So, I say, "Roman, a spirit of excellence gets rewards. A spirit of excellence sets one up for success."

He then does his absolute best, and his best is good enough for me as well as God.

4. *Reward with encouragement and give lots of recognition.*

Encourage the tasks that they're doing, their attitude with chores, the manner of excellence in working, and the order in how they're working. Later on in life, these attributes are the very skills that will get them promoted and earn them raises, that will cause growth in their businesses and help their marriages survive. Understand that it's not about the dishwasher or the laundry, per se, it's about attitude. It's about order. It's about excellence and efficiency in working.

One day I taught Roman how to load the dishwasher. (All of them had learned to unload the dishwasher at a very young age, but loading the dishwasher is different in that I have a particular way I like it done. I like it organized so more fits in; therefore, it's more efficient and costs less to use.)

"Roman, based on how good you unload the dishwasher, I want you to remember how you should load it."

"OK, the glasses go up here." He starts to put them in.

"Roman, look, watch this. I've got this secret little thing. When you put them all in order right here, you can fit more in."

"Oh, cool!"

Then I said, "Roman, I appreciate your attitude of wanting to learn. I appreciate your attitude with doing this. Now let's see if you can do it with excellence and I'll time you. Let's see how quickly you can get it done."

Roman is a Sapphire. He loves to play games. Everything has to be a game (that's true actually for most children). So he did it, and when Hans came home for dinner, the first thing I said in front of Roman and everyone else was, "Hans, guess what?"

"What?"

"Roman learned a new task today."

"Really? Roman, what did you learn how to do?"

"Load the dishwasher."

"Dude, that's awesome!"

We celebrated the task that he learned how to do. Will Roman have a great attitude the next time we ask him to load the dishwasher? More than likely, yes! There's also a better chance of him liking it because he received recognition for doing it well. Kids love recognition. They love encouragement. They eat it up just like you and I do.

5. Sports build character and instill responsibility.

Character building is hugely important. There were three things that my parents did for me that were amazing.

- **One, they involved me in sports at a young age.** That's where I learned about teamwork and winning. That's where I gained a little bit of confidence, even though my dad was so hostile and crazy at home. With sports and basketball, I learned much that I continue to apply in business today since it's a team sport.

- **Two, they enrolled me in a Christian school.** Therefore I was in an environment where the peer pressure wasn't as strong as in public schools to drink, have sex, or party. I wouldn't be the woman I am today or have the most amazing, phenomenal, outrageous relationship with my God if my parents hadn't put me in that school at that particular time.

- **Three, when I got pregnant in high school, my mom set me up in an apartment.** She said, "This is the last time I'm going to help you. You have to figure out how to take care of yourself. You've made an adult decision to have a baby. You've made an adult decision to move out on your own, so you're going to have to deal with adult consequences."

I called her after I was bedridden from the pregnancy and she said, "Well, I guess you're going to have to go on welfare." My mom didn't give me another dime. She didn't say, "Oh, I'm sorry you're bedridden, honey. I'll come over and take care of you. I'll bring you some food, and I'll do this and that."

You know what? It took one time standing in a welfare line for me to make the decision, "Oh, no way! Oh, no *stinkin'* way is this for me." The humiliation of going there and receiving that check was enough. A little over a year later, I started a business, and I've never earned less than a 6-figure income. Why? Because on that day, my mother did not cave in and give me money. Instead, she said, "It's time for you to take care of yourself." And boy, I figured out real fast how to make the most money I could.

Anyway, sports build responsibility and character. This is very important for future success. I use sports to groom our kids' character to eventually lead corporations and families someday. Cabe and Arika are amazing athletes. I look for the fruit that the sport is producing in them, and then I have the perfect opportunity to groom their hearts for what is to come. Often I see kids on the court with horrible sportsmanship, whimpering, whining, having bad attitudes, and totally *dissing* each other and their coach. If they win, they're happy. If they lose, they're miserable and mean-spirited, blaming everybody. (Unfortunately I've watched the parents do the same.)

I've told our son and daughter, "God is using this sport. He's using this time for you to learn how to succeed in a teamwork environment, which is what marriage, raising kids, and working a job or business is all about. It's all about teamwork!" Very few people know how to work as a team and it's very sad.

Look for the fruit in the sport. Disrespecting the coach is not acceptable. That is who they're submitted to, whether they like it, agree with it, or not. It doesn't matter; they have to go along with him or her. If they think the play was right or not, it's not for them to mention.

Before they even meet the coach, I set the stage for them to succeed by using prevention strategies. I tell them about different types of kids who will be on the team. "Listen, someday you might be coaching a team. Now tell me, do you want those kids saying, 'You don't know what you're doing?'"

"No."

"Whatever you sow into your coach now will come back to you in the future. If you want people to honor and respect you as a coach or as a leader, you need to make sure that you honor, respect, listen, and have a teachable heart."

When our son first started playing hockey at 7 years old, I told him, "Cabe, do you want to know how to get the most amount of play time that you can?"

"Yes!"

"Anything your coach tells you to do, do it wholeheartedly and say, 'Yes, sir.' Whenever they order you guys to do lines or 'suicides' (as they call them), even though you may hate them, if you do it with a spirit of excellence and the right attitude, he'll pick you to play. Why? Because people choose those they like to work with, that's why."

Look at what that is preparing him for. Think about that.

"Cabe," I continue, "Not only that, but when you go at it with all you have, he'll see that you have a strong desire and that you're driven, so he's going to play those with that attitude. Not only that, but by doing those suicide lines during practices, your skill set will increase. As your skill set increases, you're going to make first string. God sees everything we do, and He is the one who determines whether or not we will play."

Does any of this sound familiar to you? Look, everything I taught our son fully guarantees a future promotion on a future job. When he's in that job situation working under a manager, he'll respond, "Yes, sir. I'd be glad to. What else can I do?" His manager will see him working quickly and diligently with a spirit of excellence. He'll see his skills increase, and that will move him up the ladder. Even as an entrepreneur or a self-made millionaire, he won't be able to succeed without learning this lesson. "Yes, I'd be glad to," is the right response. It shows a spirit of excellence. I'm teaching our son to be teachable and coachable. Do you know how many unteachable, uncoachable, pig-headed, and egotistical, arrogant numbskulls I've come across in my life? They're failing for this reason. Yes, they may be making short-term money now, but often their lives are full of disasters.

I don't want to raise a son who makes a lot of money, but has a disastrous life on his hands. I don't want him to die prematurely or be divorced three times with kids who hate him. A lot of that nonsense is happening today. But that's not what I'm grooming our son for. I'm grooming him for "balanced" success. We're using sports to groom him to honor his coach. "I'd be glad to." Then, go at the drill whole-heartedly whether in agreement or not. "Yes, sir." The coach will use those he likes and who are the best. The guy who's going to be the best is the one who works the hardest, even if he starts with no skill.

Our son was one of the youngest and one of the better players in the league for his age division. This has been true in every sport he's played.

Make sure that you're grooming your children's hearts properly. If you're yelling at the coach, you're teaching them to do the same. You're teaching them to dishonor authority. You're teaching them to disrespect the coach. Please listen to me. One of the biggest hindrances I've seen in adults is that they're unteachable know-it-alls. If you don't agree with the coach, never say anything disrespectful about the coach in front of your kid. You will cause your son to lose respect for his coach, and that will not help his performance.

We have to groom in our children a teachable heart—one that is coachable, willing to learn, and willing to submit to authority and the chain of command. There is a chain of command even when you're self-employed. At the top of that chain is God. You ultimately answer to God, and He's the only One who determines, based on your spirit of excellence, diligence, and skill set, whether you'll get promoted, whether your business will increase or not. It's a 50/50 deal.

"I can't stand my coach. He's an idiot." Whoa! Hold on a second there. Don't overlook this statement, even if you agree with what they're saying. Otherwise you're teaching your children to be uncoachable. Look at your life right now. How much trouble have you gotten into, and how many ruts have you been stuck in because you weren't coachable, teachable, and wouldn't listen to anybody? What kind of disasters have you experienced in your life as a result? Maybe you have been in a rut for 20 years because you stopped learning 25 years ago. Think about it.

Groom a teachable heart in your kids. Use music lessons to groom them. This works too. I've used guitar lessons to groom Arika. Isa, a recording artist who lives near us, is helping to groom Arika's musical talents. I told Arika, "Anytime you're with Isa, don't you dare say, 'Oh, yes, I know that. Oh, yes, I know how to do that.' Don't you dare," I said. "With somebody of that level of expertise, don't you dare size yourself up to prove that you're her equal, because you're not. Not yet! She'll teach you how to surpass her if you pay attention and have a heart that's says, 'What can I learn from you? OK, how do I do that? Thank you so much. What can I learn next?'"

Imagine if you were groomed to be teachable. Imagine the wealth of wisdom that would reside in you.

Do you know what made a massive change in my life? Twenty years ago, I had somebody knock me upside my silly head—figuratively. A multimillionaire confronted me in front of a bunch of people after I said to him, "I've got a great idea."

He said, "You're so stupid!" He publicly humiliated me and went on to say, "That's what's wrong with you 98-percenters. You think you've got it all together. You think you know it all, and yet, here you are with somebody making half-a-million a month who could show you how to be successful. But you're too busy sizing yourself up to learn anything. How much do you make?"

"Well, I'm just kind of getting started," I answered.

"Well, how much am I making?"

"A half-a-million a month!"

"Then sit down, and shut up, and pay attention," he said, "because your ideas have made you broke. My ideas are making me $500,000 a month. As soon as your stack is as big as mine, then talk to me."

That was the best day of my life! This happened 20 years ago, and since that time, I've been studying successful people. I've been humbling myself to people who are:

- Successful in marriage. "Man, how have you accomplished that? That's great! Can you give me your secrets?"

- Successful in raising kids. "Gosh! How did you raise that successful kid? Can you tell me? What did you do?"

- Successful in business. "OK, can you tell me, how are you doing that?"

I humble myself instead of sizing up and competing with them or thinking I know it all. I ask, "What are you doing that's working for you?" That's my heart. Show me. Teach me; and that's what I want our kids' hearts to be like as well. People who think they know it all and are the only ones who can do everything have an ego trip that heads straight to a road block. It leads straight into a rut. Growth stops whenever you think you're the only one who can or the only one who should. If you think you have it all together, that's a big-time road block.

Children, and adults, need to have humble hearts to learn from successful people and to constantly strive for excellence.

6. Good attitude after the sports activity or play.

Having a good attitude after the game is finished or the play time is completed is very important. For example, as previously mentioned, when Arika returned from a trip helping children who were hungry and had poor living situations in Mexico a couple of years ago, she started treating her brothers poorly. I asked, "What's going on? I know that your heart wants to be in Mexico with all of those homeless and hungry kids. Would you like to someday go back and help them again?" Her response was an obvious "yes."

"Arika you earned the privilege of going on that trip by being trusted with how you treated all the little kids who are around you every day. If you want an opportunity to go again, then you must be trusted again. Treating your brothers with honor and love is one of the ways to gain the privilege again. Remember, if you can be trusted with what is in front of you, then you will be given more. The more that you want is loving on more kids around the world and helping them in any way you can. A good attitude toward your own flesh and blood should at least be equal, if not more than toward others. You should be showing them love, unconditionally wanting to help, encourage, and lift them up. This is what you've just finished doing in Mexico for a week. I know your brothers are annoying, but the bottom line: if you can be trusted with what's in front of you, then you'll be promoted to something bigger.

Guess what? Her attitude changed in a heartbeat. Her motivation is to serve others who are less fortunate than herself around the world, but she had to know that her training started in our home. Home is her training ground. Being trained up to love the unlovable, which are her brothers at times, was her challenge. And she rose to the occasion. Since then, she has been to Mexico two more times, the Philippines for three weeks, Japan for three weeks, and many other places all before the age of 16.

CHAPTER 11

STRATEGY #7:
FINANCIAL RESPONSIBILITY

*The Lord sends poverty and wealth; He humbles
and He exalts.*

—1 SAMUEL 2:7

YOUR KIDS WILL HAVE THE BEST
FINANCIAL SUCCESS POSSIBLE!

Now, let's talk about money. We teach debt elimination at our live events and have had tens of thousands pay off hundreds of millions of debt in the last five years. *Creating a Dynasty* our advanced leadership conference is a training program where we cover a multitude of topics, one of which is the wealth mindset and various concepts to develop wealth. I believe in teaching kids these concepts, also, and there's lots of different ways to do that.

You may need training yourself, so I encourage you to visit our website: www.DaniJohnson.com. Our next event will be posted there, and you'll find that it's worth the fee to attend our seminars. You'll also learn how to pay off all of your debt in the next five to seven years, including your mortgage.

Do you want your kids to struggle financially like you have? If the answer is "no," then ask yourself these other questions as well.

- Do you want them to have the burden of debt like you have?

- Do you want them to worry and stress over money?

I'm sure your answer is "no" to all of these questions. Like most parents, you want your children to have full-on financial freedom and success in every area of their lives. With the economy and the cost of housing the way it is today, this is a real concern. Many parents think, *Gosh! What are they going to do? Will they have to be a brain surgeon in order to buy a tiny shack in the city?*

As of this writing, the cost of housing has declined substantially with the downturn of the economy. But you, as a parent, have an obligation and a moral responsibility to make sure that you're grooming your kids in the area of finance, as well as in all areas of their lives. The truth is that both spouses will have to work around the clock just to purchase a small house. Parents won't even know their kids because of all the time spent away working. It's unfortunate, but it's a reality. Few mothers are raising their own kids today; rather they are being raised in daycare facilities. It doesn't have to be that way, but that's what most have chosen.

Please consider seriously the following Scripture, *"A prudent person foresees danger and takes precautions. The simpleton goes blindly on and suffers the consequences"* (Proverbs 22:3 NLT). I'm telling you the truth when I say that right now the economy and the cost of living is ridiculous and not getting any better, especially in California, New York, and most cities globally. You have a moral obligation to ensure that your kids will have the best financial success possible.

If you're not having the best possible financial success yourself, you have a moral obligation to do so for the *next generation*. Do you want to change the curse of poverty that's been on your family for generations? It's not scriptural to keep a curse of poverty on your life. Let me show you why it's there and assure you that it's definitely something that was passed down to you.

Financial viewpoints are passed down from one generation to the next. Your financial life was passed down to you from your parents, and you're living that life. What kind of example do want to be for your kids? You're in control of that. My husband and I refused to be poor, and we did whatever it took not to be.

Children need to know how to handle, manage, and make money, and when you equip yourself with the skill, you can transfer it to them.

Imagine if wealth strategies rather than poverty strategies were passed on to you—how different your life would be right now. What if debt elimination strategies were given to you at an early age? Life would be so much easier now—no question. But it still can be once you plug into our next event. Do whatever it takes to get rid of your bad poverty habits and learn how to make money, keep it, and then make it grow and work for you instead of you working for it.

Parents, this is our responsibility. The school system is not going to teach your kids how to become wealthy. Sports programs won't teach them, either. Piano lessons, your kids' friends, cartoons, television programs, videos, books—won't do it.

In the 14,000 hours of schooling you had from kindergarten to twelfth grade, how many of those hours were devoted to teaching you how to live your life with financial success? Zero! No one else is going to teach your children these principles. If they will be taught, it has to come from you. You have more influence over your children than anybody else on the planet. If you think you don't, it's just because you don't have the know-how to influence them.

In our corporation, Hans and I have influence on our employees and how they work. If we don't pull the best out of them, it's because we don't know how. Many people say, "Oh well, that's just how that worked out." Uh-uh! You reap what you sow, period, end of story.

Look at the fruit of your influence. If you are the head of an organization or managing a business as a corporate leader or a pastor of a church, what is the level of performance in your employees or congregation? The answer will directly determine your influence on them and how effective you are in your role. It's the same with your kids. If you don't feel like you have influence over them, trust me, it's a communication problem, and that's why you're reading this book—to learn how to overcome it. No one else will instill financial responsibility into them but you. So hear me out.

> *The Lord sends poverty and wealth; He humbles and He exalts* (1 Samuel 2:7).

> *For God does not show favoritism* (Romans 2:11).

> *The plans of the diligent lead to profit as surely as haste leads to poverty* (Proverbs 21:5).

The basis of what I will teach concerning finances will come from these verses, as well as from Matthew 25 regarding the Parable of the Talents. In that passage of Scripture, God gave talents of money to His servants, *each according to their own ability.*

Mechanics earn a certain amount of money according to their ability. Doctors earn a certain amount of money, according to their ability. Nurses make money according to their ability. God gives talents of money *according to each person's ability.* Check out this massive nugget of wisdom concerning money. In Matthew's account, two servants doubled their money, were allowed to keep it all, and then were blessed with more money. But one of the three servants took his one talent and buried it because of fear.

The master responded, "You're wicked. You're lazy. You're unprofitable; get out of my sight." It's important that you and your kids get this revelation.

Don't put your financial curse, financial inhibitions, and financial methods on your kids (unless of coarse you are in the 2%). If you're accustomed to saying, "We can't afford that," stop saying it. This is a hindering belief regarding money. It's an excuse, and an excuse is a well-planned lie. Teach your kids this definition of "excuse." I have.

The truth is *we can afford whatever is important to us.* If we don't have the money, we know how to get it. If one of your son's or daughter's lives depended on it, you would know how to come up with it quickly. So when you say, "We can't afford it," that makes you a victim of poverty. It is admitting that you're a victim, and you're selling that mindset to your children. Now they know how to be victimized too. They're learning how to let their checkbooks determine their lives. Make it a point never to say that again. I'll tell you what to say, instead.

Hans and I have made millions of dollars for many years, and we can afford to buy our kids every new, fandangle thing that they bring to our attention. But do we? No. "You know, Evan has an Xbox." (Or an iPod, or...you know, everything and anything that is on the market.)

"Well, that's good for Evan. Just because we have the money to buy it doesn't mean it's a good thing to buy."

"Well, you know so-and-so's got this, and so-and-so's got that."

"Man, that's awesome for them. Good for them."

Cabe is the one who comes at me the most with that kind of stuff because he's a Ruby. He's attracted to having the latest, greatest stuff in the marketplace. (He doesn't ask that often anymore.)

"Cabe," I'll say, "Let me tell you what leads to poverty and failure. It's seeing something that you must have, and on an impulse, taking it. It's not about how much money you make, Cabe, it's about how much you keep. So just because there's a lot of cool stuff out there to buy doesn't mean it's wise to buy it. Ninety-eight percent of the population is led to slaughter financially because they have to have what they see, so they make unwise financial choices."

This is a lot better than saying, "We can't afford that."

Our kids have wealthy parents, and yet you would be blown away if you knew the stuff they *don't* have. Our family wears hand-me-downs. In fact, I got a bag full of them yesterday, and they love them. Why? Because I'm teaching them how to be frugal; I'm teaching them how to be mindful where the money goes. I'm teaching them how to appreciate being wise with money. Just because you can buy it or somebody else can buy it, that doesn't mean it's a wise move. I don't want our kids to be gluttons or greedy. Those are two of the biggest hindrances in the vast majority of people's lives.

Why are people in debt? Because of greed and bad habits. "I have to have it. I have to have it. I have to!"

Just think about this. You've just received a credit card bill for a total of $5,000. Right now, you have no idea how you spent that much money. *What did you buy that would rack up that amount?* Well, look in your closet. You have stuff in there with tags still on it. The point is to choose another way to live as a good financial example so your kids don't go into debt following the road you set for them. That's what I'm trying to teach you. So saying you *can't afford it* is a joke. Tell them instead, "Just because they have it doesn't mean it's wise for us to have it."

YOUR KIDS WILL SPEND THE WAY YOU SPEND

Your children are watching you, so be wise. They're watching and listening, and believe me, they see the excess. They see you with a credit card buying another black shirt. They see the full pantry and you at the grocery store, again. They see you watching infomercials and saying how cool the item is, and then they watch you pull out the credit card and purchase it. They see the boxes showing up with all of that stuff, and guess what? It makes them think they're also entitled.

Do you want a big wake-up call? Go through your check register. It will show you the things that are important to you. Where you spend money is what's most important to you because that's where you've put your focus. Be wise with your money. Don't raise your kids with a poverty mentality. Realize that 98 percent of the population is dead-broke at the age of 65. This is how the curse of poverty passes from one generation to another, over and over and over again. It has to stop, and you can help it stop now.

We're a nation that's trillions of dollars in debt. That's the horrible sign of greed and gluttony—"I have to have the best house, the best car, the best this, and the best that."

We have chosen to raise our kids to be frugal, to keep their money, and to invest it wisely. They are not being taught to spend it foolishly. Now I'm not saying we don't do fun things because we do. We just came back from a beautiful vacation in the tropics, and this is what we told them: "See, because we don't spend money in all the other foolish areas, we can go around the world doing big things and fun things. We save a percentage of money in order for this to happen."

When we took them to Australia, we said the same thing: "Guys, can you believe how God has blessed us because we've been wise with the small things? He has blessed us with an abundance of more, and that abundance gets us vacations like this. Isn't this better than an Xbox?"

"Yes!"

TITHING AND GIVING

Many of you still have a very hard time tithing and giving. I've come across many stingy adults, and I know my Bible says that *stinginess leads to poverty* (Prov. 11:24 paraphrased). We all know kids who don't like to share; they're totally stingy. *Stinginess leads to poverty*, so when it comes to tithing, we are big believers. In fact, we take 10 percent off of our corporation's gross profits and sow it into God's work. This means that at least 30 percent of our net profits go toward that.

Our kids are strongly encouraged to tithe 10 percent of whatever they earn to an orphanage, to feed and clothe the poor, or to combat the sex trade. It's mandatory that they give it somewhere; so they take their 10 percent and give. They've learned that this money that they have been given is not theirs. It's God's money, and He trusts them with it and watches to see what they'll do with it.

If you can be trusted with a little bit, God will give you more.

Clearly the Bible says that a giving spirit leads to prosperity and stinginess leads to poverty. If you want them to prosper, teach them while they are young how to give to places that take care of the poor, the cold, the hungry, and the homeless—people less fortunate than they are. Make sure that they understand the concept that the money is not theirs; it's on loan from God and He's watching to see what they're going to do with it.

"You can take 10 percent and spend it however you want to, but the first 10 percent goes to helping the poor and those in serious need. The rest goes into an asset account." This is what we tell our kids.

GIVE YOUR KIDS AN ASSET ACCOUNT

This is the wealth strategy we've developed for our children. Each of our children has an asset account. The asset account produces income. When it reaches certain high points, we match them. For example, when they get their first $100, we match them $100. When they've earned and deposited $1,000 in their account, then we match them $1,000.

When Hans initially set up the accounts for our kids, he told them, "This is not to buy toys. This account is not to buy a car when you're 16 because a car is a liability. It's something that costs you money and depreciates yearly. This money is for your first house or something that appreciates in value, which is called an asset." So our kids have money saved right now for their first house or whatever the *asset may be*.

How do they earn money? They earn it in points by doing chores. They earn it in points when going the extra mile with certain chores and doing something they were asked to do. I reward initiative heavily because that's what causes people to get promoted in life. Going the extra mile grows somebody's business. In marriage, a husband or a wife who goes the extra mile—talk about the love thing overflowing? Not being asked to do something and then doing it anyway—that's awesome!

Kids with no initiative won't go far. I've also seen this during all the years of having companies and building organizations. People with no drive or initiative don't go very far. Without the desire to succeed, people don't progress. But the ones with initiative, those looking to fill a need and wanting to go the extra mile, they are the ones in line for the next promotion. "How can I help this person? Oh, my manager's desk is a mess. I'll clean things up." Boom! Great things happen.

Our kids are learning that it's important to have an asset account. They earn money for initiative. They earn money for excellence. They earn money for doing chores, going the extra mile, organizing a closet, whatever! I'll invent things that they can earn money doing, and then they make the deposits.

Arika works in our office. Her money is deposited into an asset account, and that asset is money on loan from God. This is what I teach them: the money that they're being entrusted with is to use wisely. Their money will give birth to more money. When they purchase a house, it has the opportunity to increase in value, which means the initial investment gives birth to more money.

This is what we teach our kids early. That toy will break or you'll lose interest in it. This means the toy loses money *and* its value. Spending money on a Nintendo, an Xbox, or more videos is also a liability.

"Oh, I earned this money. This is what I wanted to buy."

"OK, let's see if it qualifies as a valuable thing to buy. Will this item break?"

"Uh-huh."

"Will you lose interest in some of that?"

"Yes."

"Do you get bored with some of those things now?"

"Yes."

"OK. Does a video make you money?"

"No."

"Does a house make you money?"

"Yes."

"Then that's where you're going to put your money."

This lesson teaches about value and the difference between an asset and a liability. If you have no wealth strategies, then most of what I'm saying is going over your head. Many people have not been groomed on how to create wealth or a net worth for themselves. Many don't have any idea how to do this, but I encourage you to apply this strategy quickly.

KIDS NEED TO LEARN HOW TO EARN MONEY

It is important for kids to learn how to earn money. I really believe this wholeheartedly. How else can you teach them how to build wealth? Some don't want their kids earning money. But let me tell you something, how else will they learn how to handle it? If they're not learning it now by being equipped every step of the way with on-the-job training from you, do you think when they're 18 they will bother to ask? They won't. So if you teach them to earn and manage money while they're young, it becomes a habit.

Everything that I talked about in the last section about their attitude toward work, excellence, diligence, and initiative, our kids will be equipped with when entering adulthood. They'll know how to earn money, how to manage it, and how to be promoted because they already have the habit in action.

Don't complain about your job, your boss, or your financial situation, especially in front of your kids.

Many parents struggle in this area. They struggle with procrastination, work ethics, and opinions like: "I'm only going to work as much as I need to so I don't get fired, especially since they'll only pay me enough so that I won't quit." Basically, that's the mentality of today's workforce. This is the average, mediocre, pathetic life and ethics of the working majority (98 percent of the population). But it doesn't have to be that way. This mentality will only lead to poverty and give your children the wrong concept regarding work.

CHAPTER 12

STRATEGY #8:
DREAMS & GOALS

Everything is possible for him who believes.
—MARK 9:23

YOUR KIDS WILL COMPLETE THE
VISION PLACED WITHIN THEM!

Let's preface this section with another hindering belief that you won't want to pass on to your kids: "Don't get your hopes up." Suppose your child wants to act someday. But if they hear you say, "Don't get your hopes up," subconsciously, it may discourage them. Instead ask, "What has God planted in your heart to do?"

This is what I asked our kids when they were very young, and it's amazing that not much has changed since then. The occupations may have changed a bit, but the calling hasn't. Here's a prime example. I asked Micah several years ago, "Son, what has God put in your heart to do?"

"I want to be an artist."

This brings us to the next point.

245

Look for their natural strength, talents, and gifting; then, nurture it by keeping them focused on their goal.

"Mommy is going to help groom you to be the best you possibly can be. While you're in this house, my job is to train you to do what God has placed in your heart to do."

Arika wants to be a missionary. Roman wants to be an astronaut. Micah wants to be an artist, and Cabe wants to be a hockey coach. I'm not a hockey coach; I'm a business coach. But coaching I know how to do. (I'm doing that right now with you.)

Roman wants to be an astronaut, so I asked him: "Tell me why? What about that excites you?" I've asked each of them at various times these same questions.

In Roman's case, "I don't know. I just want to go beyond what other people do. I want to do something unusual, Mommy. I want to go way, way up there, and I want to get as close to God as I possibly can." Wow! Great answer!

"Awesome! Mommy's going to do whatever I can to help groom that dream in you." I bought him books on astronomy, and now the kid knows everything about the planets, and he loves it. We talk about what he has learned.

"You know, I have to get in the Air Force if I want to become an astronaut."

"Oh, really, tell me why?"

"Well, it's part of that program."

He was five years old at the time and naturally seemed to gravitate toward hearing things of that nature because God placed this dream in his heart. He constantly dresses in camouflage, and he has a warrior spirit. His dream is to go beyond what normal people will do. That's what this is about. It is to do things that others won't; to take risks that most people won't. That's what I'm grooming in him. He can become an astronaut or a powerful businessman or military officer. In his mind, the desire is the military because he has all of this military stuff. He plays battle games all the time. Mind you, this son has also been trained to battle in the Spirit because of nightmares. I've taught him how to fight the good fight of faith against all opposition. I've taught him because there's a warrior inside our son. There is a risk-taker and a history-maker in him.

Look for natural strengths in your children. We first discovered that our youngest son had an artistic gifting on him when he was about a year old. Micah painted his bedroom 23 times with poop, I'm not kidding you. I'm telling you, he would wake up from a nap with poop in his diaper; take it off and paint the textured walls with it. He expressed himself through his hands.

When he was 2, I found him on the computer clicking around and figuring it out. Obviously, he couldn't get on the Internet, but he knew how to change the screen saver at that age. That's an inquisitive mind. Micah used to go into one of my bathroom drawers and grab all of my hair ties, scrunches, and barrettes, and put them in his hair. That's an artistic expression in him. He'd also take all of those things and hide them. In fact, he once hid my mother's keys and we have yet to find them. We've even moved and still haven't found them.

This also is a very creative expression in our son. We know he has to express his creativity, so we're shepherding that instead of stifling or demeaning it. "You won't be able to do anything with that gift. Have you heard of starving artists?" So many ignorant parents and teachers have spoken those words and have squashed a dream in a child.

There's more than one way to skin a cat, and today artists can work at many innovative and productive positions. Graphic designers, architects, desktop publishers, animators, illustrators—these careers earn great money. Micah could own a graphic design firm. In other words, there are all kinds of occupations he can work in to express his artistic side and earn a living. It all depends on how we help to groom this gift of his.

To groom this artistic ability, I think, *OK, what will he need?* Then I call his creativity out by treating him as though he's already a successful artist.

Ask yourself this same question: *What do my children need in order to fulfill their destiny and purpose?* Then get them books and videos that support their goals and dreams. Take them to museums or locations that will add to their knowledge. Find their natural gifts, nurture them, and call them out.

Who do they need to become to achieve what's in their heart? Groom them in that direction.

For your child to accomplish their dreams and goals, you need to understand the big picture of their motivation. Then groom character and personal development within them.

When Micah was 4 or 5, he's now 10, he amazed us whenever we would take him to a museum or art gallery in San Francisco. At one art gallery, all of our kids were so excited about what they were seeing. "Cool! Wow, dude! Awesome! Look at this!"

But Micah grabbed my heart. He said, "Mom, I just can't believe this. Mom, I just can't believe this."

"What?" I asked.

"This is so beautiful."

"Really? What do you like about it?"

"Look at the colors. Look at the lights. Mom, it makes me feel funny inside. Oh, Mom, come here. Oh, Mom, I can't believe this one." He stopped and looked at every painting and every sculpture.

I asked, "Micah, do you like this?"

"Yes Mommy!"

"Do you want to do this someday?"

"Yes, but Mommy, I'm not that good." Already doubt was entering his 5-year-old mind. "But I'm not that good. I don't know if I can."

I got down on my knees, looked in his eyes and said, "Look at me, Micah. God has already put it in your hands to do this. You were created and designed with everything it takes to do this. All you have to do is seek God and work diligently with the right attitude. Take risks with that, and God's hand will be on your hand. You'll do even greater things with His hand on yours than what you see here. Micah, what's Philippians 4:13?"

"I can do all things," he says.

"...through who?"

"...through Christ."

"You can't do this on your own, Micah. You can't go out and create this by yourself. But with God, He will show you visions of things you'll draw, paint, and create that are far bigger and better than this. He will also create opportunities for you to learn from other artists that He has given the same gift to." Look at how doubt started to slip in on a 5-year-old because of being intimidated while looking at great works of art. You as the parent can help to build their faith and encourage them to believe that they can achieve what is in their hearts to do.

Remind them of their goals and help them stay on track.

Tell them often what is to come. Remind them that house chores are preparing them to be the hockey coach, the warrior, the artist, or the missionary someday. But if they can't be diligent now, how will they be diligent in completing long-term projects like a painting or a sculpture. All of this character-building has to be developed within them. Keep reminding them of their dreams. Keep helping them make decisions toward their goals.

- In regard to Micah, I'm preparing our artist to work with excellence and diligence.

- "If you can be diligent with your chores now, then you will be trusted with bigger and better things like diligently completing a painting or a sculpture.

- I'm preparing our leader to learn leadership skills by interacting with siblings, classmates, and teachers at school.

- "OK, awesome! God's going to use your brothers and sisters to teach you how to lead others to greatness."

We believe in wisely investing into our children.

We believe that they should be trained to be responsible with what they have. For example, Arika wanted a guitar. Since we had a piano already that was given to us, we started with piano lessons and told her if she was diligent practicing with her little keyboard, then we would invest more money into her music as well.

Please don't just throw money at these things that they want to do. They need to prove to you that they're really interested, that they will be diligent and responsible. It's a big mistake to throw a bunch of cash at every little whim that they're hyped up to do. This teaches them poor money management skills.

Instead, help them set goals. If you have certain character-building activities that you want to groom into them, set a goal—maybe two or three of them.

"Arika, about keeping your room clean...Listen, I know you want to go on this mission trip. Can you diligently keep your drawers and your closet organized? I'm trying to groom this in you to make your life simpler and easier for the long run. If you can handle this task, then you'll be rewarded with the mission trip. On a mission trip there are two types of travelers: (1) the traveler who is a pain in the backside for the leaders because they are messy, unorganized, and leave their stuff everywhere; and (2) the traveler who honors their leaders by keeping things orderly, so when it's time to do an activity, that person is ready and not imposing their filth on anyone else. So you pick what kind of traveler you want to be. That's certainly determined by whether you get an invitation to return."

Last, encourage them to believe that they can.

There are two things that children must do: (1) Believe, and they will receive, and (2) Learn the task now because it won't fall out of the sky. We live in a generation that chases fantasies. It drives me crazy. Twenty-five percent of our nation believes that winning the lottery is their retirement plan. This is total irresponsibility.

Teach your children to ask God and believe that it will happen, as well as learn the right skills now to succeed. It will be beneficial for them in all areas of life.

> *Ask and it will be given to you; seek and you will find; knock and the door will be opened to you* (Matthew 7:7).

Teach them to ask. That's what I demonstrated with our son, Micah. "You need to ask God. You need to remain in God and His hand will be on your hand. When you're on that canvas and painting that picture, He's going to give you visions of what that is."

Teach your kids to gain more ability. (The abilities attained in sports and schoolwork are skill development and absolutely necessary.)

Two things lead to success and promotion:

1. **Believe.** Without faith, as I told you before, it is impossible to succeed in anything. Faith pushes through opposition, adversity, and trouble. It is certain that whatever is hoped for will come to

fruition; it is just a matter of time. This is non-negotiable, so do not give up.

2. **Skills**. They need to be skilled in order to get it done. We need to demolish this nonsense of just sitting around and hoping instead of improving skills and working with a spirit of excellence. Improve your skills and work with excellence and you have a promotion coming.

CHAPTER 13

STRATEGY #9: NUTRITION

YOUR KIDS NEED TO BE HEALTHY!

Nutrition is so important because, as parents, you're laying the foundation for either good health or future health problems for your children. I know if your son or daughter dropped dead at 25 of a heart attack, you would be mortified. But I can tell you that 100 percent of heart problems—stroke, heart disease, and cancer are all linked to poor nutrition. Today, Australia and the United States lead the world in having the most obese children. This problem is out of control.

When I was in high school more than 20 years ago, there was probably just one heavy kid. Now, it's reversed. There's maybe only a few thin kids. It blows my mind that today's youth is so obese. What we usually see are heavy parents with heavy kids and the excuse, "Well, that's just the way we're built." If that's your choice OK, but don't make that choice for your children.

Please, consider what I'm about to say. I used to be overweight, so I know what it's like to struggle with weight gain. As I told you before, my sisters were 300 pounds each and my mother 280 pounds. Obesity runs in our family, but I made a nutritional choice to stay away from the habits that lead to obesity, and I take a number of different supplements, so my weight problem has disappeared.

My oldest child has a different biological father from the other four. Her father comes from a very thin family. I mean very, very, very thin family. They are tiny, petite people and no one in their family has a weight problem. But our daughter was raised by adoptive parents who were overweight. Their lifestyle consisted of frequently eating macaroni and cheese, Top Ramen, and McDonald's. They were so busy making lots of money that their priorities were out of order. Life wasn't about the family because they were so busy working. They never had dinner together as a family except for Thanksgiving or Christmas, and dinner was prepackaged foods. My daughter didn't grow up eating fruit or learning how to make healthy choices for her body. She drank sodas and ate Costco muffins, candy, and chips. So she's always been a heavy girl and now she's a heavy young woman.

I've taught her how to be OK with who she is and to make mature, healthy decisions. When she came to live with us permanently at age 16, during the first month she lost 30 pounds because we don't have soda or juice in our house. We also don't have much sugar, so her choices for eating were only healthy foods. Every day we ate as a family with healthy choices for breakfast, lunch, and dinner. She didn't have to diet because she naturally lost weight after one month of living our dietary lifestyle.

Hans doesn't have weight problems in his family line, either. So, why is it that our four kids are lean, mean, and very healthy machines? We don't even have a family doctor (that's how infrequently we see a doctor). Our kids have been taking supplements since they were babies. They've always eaten fruits and vegetables and know how to make wise choices.

I realize that not all obese cases are from gorging oneself. I know there are obese people with a metabolism problem because of many years of yo-yo dieting. Their metabolic system says, "Forget you, buddy. I'm going to store everything you put in me." I'm not trying to trivialize this. I understand that there are health problems that also lead to obesity. But I also know that nutritionally, in most cases, this can be fixed. You're hearing from a former overweight person from an overweight family.

One of our kids has a weight problem and grew up nutritionally poor and four others don't have weight problems and grew up making wise, nutritional food choices.

Here are some of the guidelines we use:

1. Sugar and eating dessert is once in a while.

Eating dessert or sugary food is not customary in our household or a nightly habit. Dessert is rewarded maybe once a week or twice a month for birthday parties, but always in moderation. I groom our children specifically with moderation in mind. I have a personal responsibility to lead by example, and I don't want any regrets ten years from now with a bunch of health problems. This doesn't guarantee that they won't have any, but I'll guarantee you this, there's a whole lot more health problems associated with people who don't eat right and/or supplement—we all know this. This is common knowledge. There's no guarantee that you'll live longer, either. There's no guarantee that you won't have cancer, but your odds of beating stroke, heart disease, and cancer increase with a healthy lifestyle.

2. Snacks need to be healthy.

Teach your children how to make good choices. For example, anything that comes in a box is typically not a healthy snack. Pretzels are an exception, especially if you buy organic pretzels because they don't contain a lot of harmful chemicals and nasty fats. But our kids like to eat fruit. They don't eat those weird, synthetic-type fruit snacks. Instead, they eat delicious fruit or raw veggies and they love them. These make great little snacks.

When our kids visit someone else's house, they see juice, chocolate milk, and soda—stuff that's never at our house since we only drink water. One of my friends is called the "goodie-girlfriend" because every goodie imaginable is in her pantry. When our kids were young and got a little taste of that, they would ask for juice instead of water when they returned home. (This is not the case, now. All of our kids love water and drink lots of it.)

I'd have to say, "Listen. Check it out. We have God's juice. Look. It's clear and sweet and nourishes and strengthens your entire body."

I would have to sell them on water each time they returned home, even though this is all they ever drank, even as babies. I never gave our babies juice. It's nothing but sugar and gets them addicted when they're six months old. I refused to raise them that way since I was addicted to sugar, was anorexic, and almost crossed over the bulimia line. I definitely had an eating disorder at one time, and although I don't have those problems today, I discourage anyone from walking in that fashion. It may lead your kids down that unhealthy path as well.

So after they returned from my "goodie" girlfriend's house eating chocolate chip cookies and other junk, I'd say, "OK, cool! Once in a while is fine, but once in a while is only at her house." Does that stop them from asking?

"Can I have that? Can I have this? Mommy, I'm hungry. I really want some ice cream."

"Well, you know what? I'm sorry but ice cream is not quite on the agenda. However, are you hungry?"

"Yes."

"Good. There are apples."

"I don't want an apple."

"Well, then you're not that hungry."

Ten minutes later, "Mom, can I have some ice cream?"

"Are you hungry?"

"Yes, but I don't want an apple."

"Then you're not that hungry."

Ten minutes later, guess what they have in their hand? An apple, because I consistently help them make good choices. I don't even have to tell them to eat it. I don't have to say "no" to junk food at all. Their minds and their bodies are not accustomed to it so they don't long for it. Instead, they make natural choices that are healthy for them.

Here's another thing. I already said that sodas and juice create addictions because sugar is addictive. Studies have proven this. Giving your children juice when they're young begins an addiction for soda and coffee. You're probably thinking, *"Dani, that's extreme."* The facts are what they are. It's the same jolt. Sugar jacks up their adrenal glands and their insulin levels, which lead to obesity and/or diabetes. Fat, bad food choices, tons of fast food, all lead to diabetes.

Sugar is a once in a while treat. It's not a daily thing. It's not a normal custom in our home.

3. We believe in family dinners.

I believe in the family preparing a good healthy meal together in the kitchen. I believe in all of us sitting down at the same time, talking about our day, getting to know each other while eating.

4. We supplement.

Unless you're going all-organic, today's food quality is so poor that the nutritional value is absent. But that's not a reason to pick up a bag of potato chips. Just supplement and eat as well as you can and teach this to your kids. Instead of a bag of chips, make popcorn, not microwave popcorn because of the chemicals. Microwave ovens kill everything that's put in them. Get an air popper, some organic butter, and some sea salt. Those are healthy natural choices that we make so the body can break them down easily.

I spent a lot of years in the nutrition business, but I'm not trying to sell you any vitamins or supplements. I'm just telling you about the need to supplement. I won't reveal what I use, so don't even call to ask. But I encourage you to supplement; get your kids started young, and teach them about the benefits. (Cabe was swallowing big "horse" pills when he was 18 months old.)

When they get sick, which is not even yearly, we pray first, and then we swallow garlic caplets, aloe vera, and other herbs that help heal the body. This way our children are learning how to take care of their bodies.

Let me add that cheap vitamins from the store are not recommended, you're better off not taking anything. Instead, buy good quality supplements. The best that I've seen largely come from private distributors.

You don't have to become a nutrition freak to give your children a healthy start in life; however, you will need to consciously make wise choices for them in order to give them the best possible shot at a long, healthy life by teaching them a healthy lifestyle that they will pass on to their kids. I promise the changes you make here will be good for the whole family.

CHAPTER 14

FINAL POINTS FOR PARENTS

GROOMING YOUR KIDS FOR SUCCESS IS POSSIBLE!

These are some final points that I'd like to share:

1. Don't keep track of your children's wrong-doing.

Don't remind them of their failures and their mistakes. You only want to gird them up to make better choices. Never say, "Hey, remember what you did last year? You better not ever do that again." If you keep reminding them of their failures, they are going to fail again. Forgive them for the mistakes that they've made. Make sure your heart is clean toward your kids so that you can groom them properly.

2. Don't put your barriers and fears on them.

Parents have a tendency to do this. They pass their fears down, as well as their poverty spirit and lack of vision. But don't do this to your kids. It's not fair. Instead, pull the best out of them. Pull their dreams out of them and spur them on.

3. Respect and honor your spouse in front of your kids.

I've failed at this so many times, and I've certainly paid the price for it. Division surfaces when a parent talks badly behind the spouse's back or when your kids hear you say, "I don't know why he does that. You know, it's just ridiculous how he.... Oh, he makes me so mad!"

When your daughter sees and hears this, you are training her to someday dishonor her husband, too; to talk badly behind somebody else's back, even her boss's. This is what you teach them. A wedge is driven into the family that causes division and dissension and leads to mutiny in the household. It's very important that you respect and honor your spouse, especially in front of your kids. If you have a dispute, handle it behind closed doors where they don't see or hear what's going on. That way all your children see is that you're honorable to each another.

4. Live a "balanced" life.

Don't sacrifice your children for your work and your dreams; include them. If you don't, they will resent what you do and why you're doing it, and they'll go in the opposite direction.

Children are being daily sacrificed on ministry and business altars. Their parents' dedication to their ministry caused their children to be and feel neglected. I have strong feelings about this because I've witnessed sad outcomes.

The same is true for business. I've seen many kids growing up with wealthy, driven parents who end up hating the very concept of work. They hate money and hard-working people. They rebel and do anything in the opposite direction just to make a point. We've all seen this happen, and so it's important that you live a balanced life. Your kids should know that they matter more to you than your work and your dreams. So include them, and have conversations with them about it.

Please don't neglect them verbally, emotionally, mentally, or spiritually. Even if you're in ministry, you have to make sure that your household is the priority. Take care of them first. This is supported biblically. In First Timothy 3, the Bible advises to appoint bishops and deacons in the Church after "looking at their family. Does his wife or children honor and respect him? Because if he cannot manage his household, how much more can he manage the Body of Christ?"[1] He can't.

Unfortunately, this is where people in that line of work fail miserably. Although it sounds like a wonderful thing to do and, "Oh, I'm such a good person because I'm doing this," the bottom line is, if you fail to manage your household by raising kids who are respectful, you've botched it. But if you honor and respect them by not neglecting them, then you'll succeed. That's how important time management and prioritizing is.

Creating a Dynasty, our advanced three-day training seminar, teaches time management skills. Two hours are spent just on that subject alone, specifically how to run a business/career and family all at the same time. I've managed my time successfully for the past 13 years since I received the revelation that my first responsibility was to my God, then my spouse, my children—and then my work. Since that time, our corporations and finances have grown exponentially.

I encourage you with this message: if you can be trusted with the things that you have right now, God will multiply your endeavors![2] He'll help you become more efficient; you'll download ideas and strategies from Him that will totally blow your mind. So, please, don't sacrifice your kids. When you are at home, be with them.

Making your kids your priority is taking care of His business.

5. Keep proper order!

The kids don't come before the spouse. It's God—spouse—kids. Guard against your children driving a wedge between you and your spouse. God hates division and dissension. (See Proverbs 6:19.)

Here's an example of division in the home:

Your daughter comes to you and asks, "Hey, can I go to the dance tonight?"

"Yes, sure; that's totally fine with me. Go ask your father." He answers, "No." This makes the father the bad guy, and this is absolutely wrong. Now the daughter has resentment in her heart for her father and Mom becomes the hero. This is not a successful plan for raising kids. It's not a successful plan for your daughter to learn how to raise her kids or how to honor her spouse someday.

Let me tell you about one of the biggest struggles I've had in my life. It has not been our business or our kids; my biggest challenge was learning to honor and respect Hans, the man of the house. Honoring him was not happening in our home, and my husband didn't deserve to be treated that way. This was a major challenge because I wasn't taught this skill; neither did I have an example of it being modeled during my childhood. That's why it's mandatory that you, as a parent teach by word and example this important skill. Your children must learn how to honor their future spouse by watching your example.

So what's the answer for your daughter when she asks, "Can I go...?"

"You know what? Let me talk it over with Dad and we'll let you know what we decide. Just be prepared for a yes or a no, and your attitude about our decision will determine if you'll be able to go in the future."

See how simple that was, and there's no division in the household.

6. Ask your children for forgiveness if you're guilty of anything just revealed to you.

Do this now and whenever you know that you blew it. Don't be egotistical and arrogant with them; otherwise you're teaching them that skill and they will eventually treat you that way. Humble yourself whenever you've responded in anger toward them. Say, "Mommy is so sorry. Please forgive me. I love you, and I did not honor you the way I responded."

Any time I make a mistake with them, I say this. Even if I raise my voice to Hans or I've been a goofball in some other way, I say, "Mommy did not set a good example. Please forgive me for what you heard come out of my mouth."

Don't let things go without those words of forgiveness being spoken.

7.   *Respect, honor, love, and encourage them unconditionally.*

Encouragement is your best tool for pulling the best out of anybody, so *encourage* what you see. (I know that I mention this word quite a bit.) Also, you want to honor them by preparing them for success. Before you go into a public place, prepare them for that. When you're leaving a place, give them a five-minute warning so that they're not set up for failure, but for success. Tell them how to respond and encourage them when they've done it right. Look for any opportunity to encourage the good that they're doing.

8.   *Contend in prayer for their future.*

Pray to God for your children's future, salvation, and future spouses. When I found out I was carrying a son, I began to pray for his future wife. I pray for Arika's future husband. I pray for their relationships with others. I pray for their relationship with God. I pray for their success. I pray for their vision. I pray daily for their lives. I encourage you to do the same. It's the best investment of time you could ever make.

9.   *Persist because it's worth it.*

Many times I've been so frustrated and tired because of constantly correcting, refereeing, and encouraging. But I promise you, someday you'll look back from an easy state (like I'm doing right now). But there were times when I wanted to quit because they were all so young and it was just so constant. I know what that feels like; I do. But I promise you, a point is reached when things start to get easier. Grooming them while they're young means it will be a pleasure enjoying them later as young, groomed adults. They'll be a pleasure to hang out with, and they will actually speak life into you.

Roman speaks into my life almost daily. "You're the best Mom."

"Why do you say that?" I ask.

"Because you love God, and you honor Him, and you teach people about Him."

"Ah, thank you, Roman."

Micah says, "Mom, you're as beautiful as an angel."

Oh! They speak into my life in the moments when I really need it. They have learned how to encourage.

Arika blesses me so much. It's amazing the kind of young woman she has turned into. But in the beginning it was hard. Now I spend much time praying, thanking God for blessing us with her and the wisdom and knowledge of how to raise her. I am so thankful that what the Bible says has worked. It blows my mind.

Arika will come to me at times and say, "Mom, I'd love to go to the youth conference. If that's not OK with you, that's totally fine. I will understand, and I will honor whatever your decision is."

And on the way there, she'll say, "Mommy, thank you so much for giving me this opportunity. I promise you, I'll return closer to God, and I'll come back with a message to give you."

Did I have to ask her, "What should you say to me? You need to thank me." In the beginning I had to. We'd take them to a restaurant and ask later, "Guys, what should you say?" Or, we'd take them to a movie and ask again, "Guys, what should you say?"

"Thank you, Mommy, for taking us. Thank you, Daddy for taking us out to dinner. Thank you so much for this."

We've had to teach them to be thankful and grateful. We've had to teach them not to be jealous. We've had to teach them not to judge. Now they are sweeter than sweet. Disciplining is rare now. Corrections are rarer—it's more verbal than physical now. So I promise you, persist. It will be worth it, and your children will turn into some of your closest friends, people that you will love to be around.

10. Speak life into their potential.

Look at their special talents and bring out the best in them. "You can do it. I believe in you. You're awesome. You're doing an amazing job!" (See there, I'm not even talking to you and that was stimulating you.) Words of encouragement are very powerful; breathe life into your children's potential.

Don't condemn the child, but definitely bring correction to the action. Condemn the behavior, not the person. Never say to your son or daughter, "You're a *bad* girl (or boy)." That's death. If somebody believes they're bad, then that's how they're going to behave, and their life will totally depict this.

Never condemn the person—correct the behavior. Otherwise, they will experience a life of failure; they will quit before they start. They will only get so far and then fear will arise and their success will be sabotaged. I've seen a lot of horrible fruit in people's lives as a result of hearing, "You're a bad boy or girl!"

Instead say, "You're a good girl. You're a good boy and a good person, and you have a great future ahead of you. This choice you made was bad; good girls and boys make good choices. We need to fix this and make it right."

When they get in trouble, sell them on their future, where they're going, and what they're going to do, "…and this over here that you did doesn't fit into that picture." They have a desire to succeed, I promise you.

If you have botched this one up, it's not too late to go back to them and make it right. Humble yourself, ask for forgiveness, and tell them how you believe in them and their futures. Speak LIFE.

11. You don't have to sacrifice your family or health to reach success.

This has been a lie circulating for a while. I lived it and almost lost my family and my health. The truth is you don't have to sacrifice your spouse, children, or health to be successful. Time management and goal-setting will help you *keep* the right priorities, manage your time, get more out of work hours, and create additional time *and* money.

12. Become debt-free.

This is the "98 percent versus the 2 percent" rule. It's not how much you make; it's how much you keep. Your first priority: get out of debt. Your second priority: accumulate wealth. As you do, make sure to include your children in your plan. They need to understand the process and learn how to stay debt free.

13. Discipline your children.

Use the *Encourage, Correct, Encourage* method.

14. Teach how to deal with disappointment.

I deal with adults all the time who are over-reactive. I've seen people quit on marriage, business, and parenting because they weren't groomed to know that life stinks sometimes. Sometimes things don't go our way; some things have to die—that's just the way it is. If we're raising our kids under the assumption that, "Everything's always going to be positive and great," we're not preparing them for a realistic or great future.

It's important that they learn what the Book of James says about trials. Trials are part of our grooming. They build our faith, and when our faith matures, we'll lack nothing. Just don't raise them up in some fanciful, fantasy World of Disney. Life is full of hardships, and we need to teach them how to deal with them.

I used to live in that ridiculous, humanistic mindset of, "If I always think positively, if I always do positive things, then positive things are going to happen to me." That's not totally true. Sometimes we go through rough times to refine our character and to refine who we are emotionally, mentally, spiritually, physically, and financially. Teach your kids that those hard times are for refining them for what's to come. "It's a refinement process to burn off what's not good in you so that the best can rise up. It's just like gold and silver going through the refining process. It has to go through some very hard, hot, hot times before the impurities in the gold rise up."

It could mean disappointment if you answer, "I'm sorry, but you can't." If they say, "Ah, man!" and get a bad attitude about it, look at them and say, "You're going to try that again because how we deal with disappointments in life determines how many more disappointments we're going to get. Disappointment is a test. If you pass this test looking for the lesson in it, then you don't have to take that test again. Make up your mind to have a good attitude about the disappointment. Say, 'I'm going to do my best about this disappointment. I'll accept it and move on.'"

So even with big disappointments, like losing a game, say: "How you deal with this disappointment will determine what the next test is for you. So if you pass this disappointing test with flying colors, then guess what? You'll be stronger the next time and pass it, too."

Teach, mold, and groom your children how to deal with disappointments of all sizes, big and small, as soon as possible. If disappointments are allowed to rule their lives, they won't get up and try again. Do you know how many thousands of adults I come in contact with who have traded the fear of disappointments for dreaming? They have stopped dreaming, setting goals, and going after a vision because they're afraid of being disappointed and discouraged. I've watched countless thousands trade the fear of discouragement and disappointments and going after what seems to be secure. The truth is there is a risk-taker history-maker in you, and there's also one in each of your children.

Let them know that staying in those places of disappointment is not an option. Let them know that they can cry out to God for help to walk in hope and faith, and then they can get up and give it their best shot one more time. That will groom them for success and pass on freedom, rather than bondage.

I believe that you can set them up to succeed and not to fail; you are to groom them by design and not by default. You can't say, "I just didn't know how" because the rule book is in your hands. How many millions of parents throughout the years have said, "I just didn't know how. Kids don't come with an owner's manual." I understand that, but we can't say that anymore. At least now this rule book provides the guidelines, and the ultimate manual is the Bible.

Let's raise men who will lead households as the priests, providers, protectors, fathers, and husbands—maybe even community leaders and politicians. Let's raise women who will honor, respect, love, nurture, and stand side by side with their man, and they will succeed together. She will be a wife, a leader, a mother, a motivator.

We need to know that we're giving it our best shot even though we don't always know how it's all going to turn out. Even God, the perfect Father, didn't have perfect kids.

You can learn to do anything. He's called you qualified because He's put children in your life. Those children are for you to groom— to *groom for success*.

ENDNOTES

1. See 1 Timothy 3:1-13.

2. See Matthew 25:21.

CONCLUSION

A prudent person foresees danger and takes precautions. The simpleton goes blindly on and suffers the consequences.

—Proverbs 22:3 NLT

In conclusion, we've covered a lot of topics in this *Grooming the Next Generation for Success* book. Let's recap.

- We talked about the differences between protection and control.

- The negative influences that are already grooming our kids.

- We talked about living in a generation where evil is considered good and good is considered evil.

- We talked about my generation being asleep. We've been slumbering and have allowed negative things to slip in.

- We've been desensitized by the marketplace and have allowed situations to get completely out of control. Now we're at a point where we're thinking it's too late: "Oh, what's the use? What can I do about it anyway?"

• We made the stand to ban TV programs and unfiltered Internet from our house. Our kids don't have cell phones, video games, or designer clothes, and believe me, this is making a big difference in their lives and attitudes.

• We talked about equipping your kids and addressed a number of different points.

• Regarding people skills, we discussed how important it is for your children to learn to honor and respect one another and everyone around them and to conduct themselves in a manner that would glorify God and honor their parents and family members.

• We discussed the power of forgiveness and how necessary it is to release bitterness and resentment immediately.

• We learned that our kids have influence. They are in a position to lead others and help others to lead. That's why we want them to have good influence and good leadership skills.

• We talked about the importance of correction and accountability. One more thing I want to add. *"A prudent person foresees danger and takes precautions. The simpleton goes blindly on and suffers the consequences"* (Prov. 22:3 NLT). Let's demonstrate prudence; foresee the danger ahead, and take precautions. Simpletons will think everything's going to be fine. They think, *Oh, it doesn't matter. It's all going to be fine. Oh, my kids are fine. Oh, we're doing a pretty good job.* Hmmm! Then he goes blindly on and suffers devastating consequences.

- Parents, let's do whatever we can to make sure that we're not simpletons. Let's take all the precautions necessary to train up our children in the way that they should go.

- We talked about prevention and how important it is to prepare your kids in advance about their behavior before they are faced with a new situation. It's called Preparation in Advance, and it sets them up for success.

- We stressed the importance of working first, then playing. If your children are allowed to spend all their time playing, they will be raised to be mediocre, apathetic, lazy, non-dreaming average kids with no vision.

- Your children can learn about wealth and debt concepts even at a young age. This mindset can be groomed into them—and you—right now. We've helped countless thousands pay off millions and millions of debt, and we've helped many generate 6-and 7-figure incomes. If you want more information about how to do those things, please visit our website at www.danijohnson.com. You have the choice to groom them for wealth or for poverty. The choice is yours.

- When it comes to dreams and goals, don't pass on negative, hindering beliefs. Ask your children what God has planted in their hearts, and then look for their natural strengths and talents.

- Nutrition and good eating habits are important to teach your children at any age. If you teach them by example, they can learn to make wise, healthy choices now and guard against poor health in the future.

We've covered a lot of territory in this book, and I hope you realize that success can belong to you and your children. You may be feeling one of two things at this point: 1) that you are already doing a great job or 2) that you have messed up beyond repair. If you feel that you have already done a great job, good for you. Please don't overlook the fact that all of us need to continue to grow; use this book as a reference for future situations that you *will* encounter. If you feel that you have messed up beyond repair, I completely understand how you feel. I have had many times in my life where I had messed up beyond repair, at least that's what I thought. Well I am here to tell you it's not true. I don't know who your god is, but I do know who mine is, and He promises to be our *Redeemer*. If we will confess to Him what we have done, He will heal what we have hurt. It's never too late. I have watched grandparents go to their adult children and make things right by confessing what needs to be and asking for forgiveness. I have watched complete transformations happen in families thousands of times. There will be a transformation in yours.

I am confident that you have this book in your hands because it is your destiny to help Groom the Next Generation. There are thousands who are with you on this same journey, all moving toward the same goal. Together we can do what needs to be done, which is *Grooming the Next Generation for Success*!

ABOUT THE AUTHOR

Dani Johnson is an internationally sought-after speaker, best-selling author, success coach, business and financial expert, and founder of Call to Freedom International, a personal achievement and corporate training company.

Dani knows firsthand what it takes to overcome adversity and succeed in life. She went from growing up in an abusive, drug-afflicted home to striking out on her own in business at the early age of 19, only to wind up destitute, homeless, and living out of her car with $2.03 to her name.

Then something changed. She went on to earn her first million dollars in just two years, by the age of 23, starting several successful companies and businesses. Since then she's committed her life to sharing with others her proven success system, empowering and equipping others with the knowledge and skill to succeed in business and life.

Dani coaches, consults, and mentors people from all walks of life—multi-millionaire executives to people struggling to get by to middle class income people—in personal achievement, career advancement, conflict resolution, business growth, leadership development, teamwork, confidence building, overcoming fear, spiritual issues, parenting and grooming kids for success, marketing solutions, executive decision making, profit strategies, relationship marketing, time management, debt elimination, and wealth attainment.

Dani has been seen on television by millions of viewers through her numerous appearances on worldwide networks including CNBC, TBN, Daystar, and PAX.

Dani is passionately dedicated to her husband, Hans, five children, and two grandchildren. She and her husband are the founders of King's Ransom Foundation, a non-profit organization dedicated to serving people in need worldwide, especially families and children. Dani and Hans believe strongly that successful people need to give back to local communities and charitable organizations that are doing God's work around the world.

OTHER TRAINING FROM DANI JOHNSON

IS AVAILABLE AT
WWW.DANIJOHNSON.COM

Grooming the Next Generation For Success
Home Study Course

Spirit Driven Success
Audio Training Series

War On Debt
Home Study Course

GEMS Mastery Program

Unlimited Success
Audio Training Series

Online Career Advancement
Training Programs

Weekly Coaching & Mentoring Calls

Live Dani Johnson Seminars,
Events & Appearances

Free Downloads, MP3s and Reports

DANI JOHNSON'S LIVE EVENTS

SEE DANI JOHNSON LIVE AND
WATCH YOUR LIFE TRANSFORM!

Here are just a few people who have been affected by attending a live event with Dani Johnson:

I was broke, homeless, living on somebody's couch with a $500/week drug habit. Within the first year of going to Dani Johnson, I completely turned my life around. I went from a ninth-grade education to making over a six-figure income. It scares me to think what would have happened to me if I did not make the decision to plug into Dani's training.

—SHANE W.

After my first Dani Johnson Live Event, I came out and made $30,000 in the first month! I am so blown away...the internal changes in me now...there's no amount of money, there's nothing that can replace that.

—GENEVA S.

Since Atlanta, only three weeks ago, we have cut $1800 a month out of our budget. Five days after First Steps, I generated $12,000 toward debt reduction!

—SHON M.

If you would like to know where you can see Dani Johnson live, go now to www.DaniJohnson.com.

DANI JOHNSON WANTS TO HEAR FROM YOU

FOR MORE INFORMATION

For more information about Dani Johnson training programs, products and seminars or to find out how to book Dani for your next event contact:

Call to Freedom International
3225 S. McLeod Drive, Suite 100
Las Vegas, NV 89121
(866) 760-8255

www.DaniJohnson.com

Additional copies of this book and other book titles from DESTINY IMAGE are available at your local bookstore.

Call toll-free: 1-800-722-6774.

Send a request for a catalog to:

Destiny Image® Publishers, Inc.

P.O. Box 310
Shippensburg, PA 17257-0310

"Speaking to the Purposes of God for This Generation and for the Generations to Come."

For a complete list of our titles, visit us at www.destinyimage.com.